# THE ROAD TRIP

## An Entrepreneur's Journey of Self-Discovery

## Other Titles by Connie Ragen Green

*Local Business Marketing: Making the Phone Ring for Businesses Everywhere*

*Kids and Money: Teaching Financial Responsibility and Values...*

*The Baseball Short Story Anthology*

*Living the Mentored Life*

*Rethinking the Work Ethic: Embrace the Struggle and Exceed Your Own Potential*

*Doing What It Takes: The Online Entrepreneur's Playbook Book*

*Blog. Broadcast. – The Trifecta of Entrepreneurial Success*

*Write Publish Prosper: How to Write Prolifically, Publish Globally...*

*The Transformational Entrepreneur: Creating a Life of Dedication and Service*

*Living the Internet Lifestyle: Quit Your Job, Become an Entrepreneur, and Live Your Ideal Life*

*The Inner Game of Internet Marketing*

*The Weekend Marketer: Say Goodbye to the "9 to 5", Build an Online Business, and Live the Life You Love*

*Time Management Strategies for Entrepreneurs: How to Manage Your Time to Increase Your Bottom Line*

*Huge Profits with Affiliate Marketing: How to Build an Online Empire by Recommending What You Love*

*Article Marketing: How to Attract New Prospects, Create Products, and Increase Your Income*

*Huge Profits with a Tiny List: 50 Ways to Use Relationship Marketing to Increase Your Bottom Line*

*...and too many more to mention!*

# THE ROAD TRIP

## An Entrepreneur's Journey of Self-Discovery

**By Connie Ragen Green**

*ISBN Paperback: 978-1-937988-51-7*
*ISBN Kindle: 978-1-937988-52-4*

*Hunter's Moon Publishing*
*http://HuntersMoonPublishing.com*

*Interior Design by Arty Crottia*
*Cover Design by Angie Ayala*

# Dedication

A road trip across the United States and back home again does not happen without the support and friendship of many people. On the days I spent hours alone in my car as I was making my way to my next destination I felt wrapped in the arms of those who were with me in spirit.

I dedicate this book to everyone who had a part in my journey, from those who were at my live event in the spring of 2015 when I first shared this idea, to those in attendance one year later when I shared it with more conviction and intent, to those who I encountered along my route during my twenty-two days of travel, as well as all of the people in my world, both online and offline who were a part of this journey before, during, and afterwards.

And to those who opened their homes to me during my travels, a special "thank you" to you for doing so. It isn't easy hosting someone you have only spent time with previously in hotels and restaurants while at conferences, workshops, and masterminds in years past, especially when they arrive on your doorstep in a fragile and vulnerable condition. You welcomed me with open arms and made my stay with you a memorable one. You were my angels.

# Table of Contents

# Foreword

I had the pleasure of meeting Connie while on a trip I was taking to London in December of 2012. My wife and sons had gone on to Athens that morning and I was to meet with a client at his office in Hyde Park before joining my family the following day. Everything was moving like clockwork until I found myself lost in the middle of Heathrow Airport and not sure which direction to turn.

Seemingly out of the shadows Connie appeared and asked me what I have come to know over the years as her signature question, "How may I serve you?"

I'll admit I fumbled about with my glasses, my passport, and a map of the airport a passerby had thrust into my hands minutes earlier before answering "I'm lost and I need to catch a flight."

Connie had great kindness for this lost stranger and it is my belief I was not the first confused soul she had encountered and comforted the way she did for me on that day. Though she had just arrived from the States and had a private car waiting for her, she escorted me to the British Airways lounge and checked me in as her guest. She rescheduled the car service and let the hotel know she would be checking in later than expected.

We talked for more than an hour that day and it would be the beginning of a friendship that has continued through the years. Our families have even become friends as a result.

And then there is my business.

Connie is more than a pretty face with a kind smile who seeks out people to serve. She is a naturally savvy businesswoman who also serves as a brilliant mentor and consultant. I have had the chance to experience her fierce competitiveness on a number of occasions and those have been ones for the ages.

First, I must explain my business. My specialization is with streaming video and live streaming within a smaller niche around sports. My clients are on six continents and those I consult with require my presence regularly. This means that I am traveling three out of four weeks each month.

Much to the dismay of my wife and young sons I do love this work and do not wish to alter my lifestyle at this stage of the game. But I was in a conundrum and it was Connie who came up with the solution that changed everything for me by the following year. My family and I are eternally grateful for her help and ongoing mentorship in this area.

The business is busier than ever these days and I am paid well for my time. Meeting with clients on their home turf is no longer a challenge. Being acknowledged as an expert in my field comes easily. None of this was possible before meeting the person who saw my situation from a new perspective.

I did not have knowledge of this summer road trip until after the fact. Not being the naturally adventurous type the furthest I have ever driven is from Toronto, Ontario, Canada to Brandon, Manitoba, Canada. We made stops in Chicago, Illinois and Minneapolis, Minnesota in the States on our way to Brandon. My parents now live in Brandon, which is the second largest city in Manitoba and sits on the banks of the Assiniboine River. The roundtrip drive was about 4,500 km (2,800 miles) and in comparison was less than half of the distance of Connie's now famous road trip, and we were two drivers, unlike Connie's solo adventure.

As to why I was lost in London Heathrow that day, I believe I'd experienced a reaction to something I ate on my morning flight in from Toronto. It left me light-headed and a bit dizzy. My wife says that I was feigning illness in order to be rescued by a beautiful woman. All kidding aside, being rescued by Connie was a Godsend at that time in my life.

I read most of this book while it was being written and hope you will enjoy it as much as I have.

~ Malcolm Hunter

# Preface

*Wouldn't take nothin' for my journey now.*
~ Maya Angelou

In the spring of 2015, at my live marketing event in Los Angeles, California I mentioned to my group that I was planning a road trip across the United States during the summer. I stated that I hoped to meet up with as many of them as possible during this time, but I do not believe anyone in attendance took me seriously. I chalk that up to the fact that I did not have the tone of conviction in my voice. Also, I did not have any specific information or details about what would occur during this proposed road trip.

A month later I was at home thinking about what I had wanted to do and decided that it just wasn't meant to be that summer. None of my students, people in my mentor program, or other participants who were present at my event ever questioned me about this later on. My idea simply vanished into thin air after that weekend.

This is what it looks like when you are not disciplined in your thinking or firm in your decision making. This is also representative of what my life was like before I left the working world and started my online business in 2006. It consisted of half-baked ideas, goals that were merely wishes and dreams, and people who took most of what I said with a grain of salt. I was wishy-washy and my results were mediocre. My life was not going where I had hoped it would go and it was all my doing. There was no one to blame for this predicament other than myself, and I was ready for the sting of taking full responsibility to sink in.

I chose not to beat myself up over this backslide and I knew my clients would not bring it up to me because they would be afraid of putting me on the spot and possibly embarrassing me. Instead, we all allowed this incident to disappear, at least temporarily. But it never left my mind as I made my way through each day, knowing that something in my life had to change.

This experience was an important one for me, as it reminded me of the difference between taking responsibility and action to achieve your goals and of allowing your goals to simply fall by the wayside. I had changed my life significantly over the past decade and was now a person who did what they said they would do. I was determined to make this situation right, and to learn as much as I could about myself in the process.

The following spring, in March of 2016, I once again announced at my live event that I would be taking a road trip that summer. But this time was different. I watched the faces of my clients and students as they listened to the details of what I was planning to do. I had dates and cities and names of those I would be able to spend time with along the way, some in attendance at my event and others far away due to prior commitments. Then we interacted as I asked them questions about how they would like to spend time with me during the time I would come through their city or town. They envisioned me sitting at their kitchen table and helping them with their website. I pictured myself getting to know their family members and sharing why I thought my student would be successful with their business. They told me where in their city they would take me so that I would understand them and their world a little better. When we discussed the intimate details of the trip it came alive for everyone. I knew they were excited at the prospect of being included in my summer road trip and relived that I was now ready to take action on this project.

Little did I know that this trip would alter my life in such a major way and that so many people besides me would be impacted. I wrote this book not only to chronicle my road trip experience but also to share how my thinking and actions shifted with each turn in the road. It was as though I earned my wings as an entrepreneur by following through with this plan over a twenty-two day period during that summer of 2016, a time that seems so long ago at times, and at other times feels like it just occurred hours ago. It is my sincere hope that you will benefit from reading this story of challenge and courage, of hope and dreams fulfilled.

# Introduction

*Tell me a fact and I'll learn. Tell me a truth and I'll believe.*
*But tell me a story and it will live in my heart forever.*
~ Indian Proverb

Starting, growing, and maintaining an online business is a dance of sorts. It involves the intertwining of your mindset around business, the experience and skills you bring to the table when you begin, and the education you are willing to pursue and implement once you have begun.

Visualize a ballerina moving through her routine in a practiced and disciplined way. She flows across the stage like a sheer silk handkerchief blowing in the wind. Enter the jazz dancer, leaping on to the stage from out of nowhere and landing with a pivot turn alongside our ballerina. He takes a measured step back and the two dance to music only they can hear and are completely unaware of an audience taking it all in.

You appear from backstage, adding to this performance with the confidence you already have and will build upon, along with an enthusiasm for creating things seemingly out of thin air and you are on your way to a life of reinvention and enlightenment.

The duality of wearing the hats of a serious professional business owner and of a wildly energetic creative can be overwhelming at times, and it is my goal and intention to help you to transition seamlessly between the two throughout each day on your way to entrepreneurial success.

I thought my road trip would be an excellent metaphor for entrepreneurship, and within these pages I will share exactly what it takes to be a successful entrepreneur on the internet while also allowing your creative juices to flow.

This road trip occurred during the summer of 2016 when I drove across the United States, from southern California to Bowie, Maryland and back home again, covering six thousand three hundred miles, visiting seventeen states, and spending time with more than a dozen friends, family members, students, and clients over a twenty-two day period of time.

It is my sincere hope that you will embrace the stories, analogies, and situations I share with you here as a way for you to better understand and fulfill your own entrepreneurial goals and desires. Keep a journal or notebook of your thoughts and ideas as you read. And, most of all keep an open mind about what is possible when you commit to becoming the creative entrepreneur you may secretly or openly desire to be as your future unfolds in front of you on the open road.

# Section One - The Plan

*Plans are of little importance, but planning is essential.*
~ Sir Winston Churchill

Planning, implementing, course correcting, and following through with a goal to completion is similar to going through a graduate degree program at a top rated or an Ivy League university; you may think you have adequately prepared for what is about to transpire, but you soon find out much of what you believed to be true has now been altered in your consciousness based on your new experiences and how you incorporate them into your present thinking.

And something that occurred a decade or longer ago becomes pivotal in your success without your expecting such a thing. But most of all, the growth you experience from such a ride will build your character in a way that cannot be duplicated by any other life experience.

There are so many moving pieces and we reach to the people and resources that we believe will help to make sense of it all.

Connecting with people we do not know is a part of this shift in thinking and acting and we struggle to know and make sense of these entrepreneurs we have allowed to invade our personal space, even if it is only that of our email inbox.

Malcolm Gladwell writes about this in *Talking to Strangers*, where he describes how we make sense of people we do not know. In our efforts to connect with the people we will serve we are inviting conflict and misunderstanding in ways that will have a profound effect on our lives and our world. It's a conundrum, to be sure. But well worth the effort, in my opinion and experience.

While I was an undergraduate student at UCLA I befriended a fellow student who was a music major. He described his experience at the end of our first quarter in this way:

"I was the best at my high school, when it came to musical performance, technique, and composition. Here, everyone was the best at their high school so it's an entirely different world. I must work harder than ever and change how I think of and define excellence in order to be the best at this new level."

After more than a decade working exclusively on the internet it was time for me to do the same in my online business as an author, publisher, speaker, and entrepreneur and I was ready to meet the challenge. But first, I needed a vehicle in which to experience this transformation. It literally became my vehicle when I decided to begin my transformation as I drove across the United States and back home again.

I wanted to take a cross-country road trip for several reasons. These included being able to see the United States in a way that I hadn't since I had driven across the country several times with my first husband during the 1980s; to be alone with my thoughts and ideas as I drove through areas so different from what I was now experiencing it would seem like a foreign country; and to visit about a dozen clients, friends, and family members along the way in an effort to get to know them better and to serve them in any way possible.

In my mind I had created an abstract drawing of what this could look like. The colors were vivid, while the shapes and forms were only partially defined. It was like the middle of a dream where someone's face slowly morphs into a plant and the sound of a familiar voice becomes an approaching locomotive.

Over the next couple of weeks I created a plan that would carry me through the best of times and the worst of times as a human being. And in so doing, my perspective, outlook, and actions would test my strength and focus. Was I a person of grit or simple someone who worked in fits and spurts and was only slightly above mediocre when it came to striving for excellence?

If I had known in advance all that I would learn and how my outlook would change during my road trip, perhaps I would have done it many years before. But I sincerely believe that we are all at the exact place in our lives that we need to be at any given time. Even though hindsight can be twenty-twenty, it's more advantageous to stay the path and allow our life experience to all unfold in due time.

This road trip was an adventure, to be sure, and one that I would not trade for anything in the world. As Maya Angelou so astutely said, "I wouldn't take nothin' for my journey now." She was speaking directly to me...and I wouldn't.

# The Open Road

*The open road still softly calls, like a nearly forgotten song of childhood.*
~ Carl Sagan

It's not quite seven in the morning on Monday, June 13, 2016 and the sun is already blazing. My Honda Pilot is carefully packed and the last thing I add is a brown paper bag of leftover snacks from my kitchen. As I start out on this road trip from my home in Santa Clarita, a suburb of Los Angeles in southern California I realize that planning this trip was a similar process to the one I used when planning to start my online business back in 2005. The sun is staring me down as I drive eastwardly down the road away from my house and enter the Antelope Valley Freeway to begin the first leg of my trip. As I drive up the ramp and merge with the steadily flowing traffic I think back to the beginning of my journey as an entrepreneur when I was just getting started.

At that time I was working as a classroom teacher in the inner city of Los Angeles. This was a career I had chosen twenty years earlier and had loved more than anything I had ever done for a living for the first fifteen years or so that I was in the classroom. I eagerly took on the challenges awaiting a first year teacher and could not believe I had waited until I was thirty years old to earn my teaching credential and begin this adventure and new chapter of my life.

In my spare time (this is supposed to be a sarcastic comment, because teachers do not have any spare time) I had run a real estate business where I worked as a broker and residential appraiser. But after twenty years of this dual life time had taken its toll. I was exhausted from working six or seven days each week for more than sixty hours the majority of the time. And even with all of these days and hours I had very little in savings. Yes, I was buying my home and was able to take a vacation every other year, but I always knew I was just a few months away from losing everything if I could not work for any reason.

And then it happened; I had a second bout of cancer at the beginning of 2003, as well as a serious work injury where I fell while attempting to hang up a bulletin board before leaving for the day, at the principal's insistence. Arthroscopic surgery to reattach my rotator cuff on my left shoulder is first. Several months later I have surgery on my left knee to repair a torn meniscus. Interspersed are my cancer treatments.

These occurrences caused me to be out of work for almost six months and the monthly worker's compensation checks did not quite cover my expenses. I found myself eating macaroni and cheese, canceling my cable service, and no longer visiting my hair stylist. Looking back, this was both a time of sadness and one of joy.

Every day I did my best to stay focused and positive while also changing my thinking and mindset to that of someone who was ready for a new life. I had no idea what that life might look like but I began a period of exploration that took me in a direction I had not expected.

I'll share lots more about this over the course of this book, but suffice it to say for now that the people I encountered, the books I read, and the experiences I took on and embraced changed my life forever. The school district wanted me to return to the classroom without the benefit of any physical or occupational therapy. I consulted with an attorney and he took my case

Four months later the Worker's Compensation Appeals Board awards me a settlement consisting of treatment in a sport's treatment center about twenty miles from my house. I am to be there Monday through Friday from seven in the morning until five in the afternoon. If I can't drive myself they will come for me and this happens a few times in the first month. I am only absent once during the nineteen weeks of treatment, and that is to see my attorney in downtown Los Angeles for a deposition. My life is slowly changing and I am getting stronger.

One day I am on a lunch break and walk over to the grocery store to buy some gum. The lady in line behind me asks me where I had my hair done. I finally realize she is referring to the gray that is growing out and I tell her it's the "poor" look. I explain that I have been out of work due to a work injury. She says "Oh" in a condescending way and turns away from me. I should have said it was done at a salon in Beverly Hills but the new me just states the facts. It feels good to be empowered in this way.

I returned to teaching on the second day of January, 2004 a new person. The principal chooses to leave the long term substitute in my classroom through the end of the school year and assigns me to a physical education teacher position. When I am not the lone adult on the play yard with sixty to one hundred twenty elementary school aged children I am assisting is various classrooms with reading and mathematics.

Soon after this time real estate prices had begun to rise and by the end of that year I had refinanced my home and put almost a hundred thousand dollars in the bank. This empowered me in a way I had not previously experienced and I was ready to devise a plan that would ultimately take me out of the classroom and into a business I could run on the internet. My future is a bright one and my vision is coming into focus.

## My Vision

In the spring of 2005 I had attended a weekend seminar titled "Double Your Income and Double Your Time Off" and it was enlightening, to say the least. There were about a hundred people in attendance and I was anxious to hear everything each of them had to share. One woman sitting several rows in front of me stood up to ask a question and held up a plastic case for everyone to see. It held a booklet and some CDs and she described it as her information product. I was mesmerized by this image and at that moment the only thing I cared about was having one of those information products as my own creation. But first I was going to have to find out more about what an information product was and how I could create one to sell on the internet.

That weekend seminar led me to sign up for a year and a half long program where I would attend more than a dozen skillfully named and described programs, each one of these being two or three days in duration on a variety of topics. There were camps and speaker trainings and seminars on changing your thinking and about earning income from a home business. There was a "warrior" camp and another advanced camp for spiritual enlightenment.

Overnight I was thrust into the world of personal development and became hungry for knowledge and experiences that would change my thinking. Of course, I soon realized that I had what I needed inside of myself already and just needed to muster the courage to get everything out to achieve the success I wanted and deserved. This series of trainings became the catalyst for massive and needed change in my life and I took it in like a hungry child would take in nourishment.

And my plan unfolded just as I had hoped it would. I could see my new mission and vision more vividly than ever. One of the weekend events had us drawing pictures of our ideal day and life and I drew images that came from someplace deep inside of me. One of these drawings was of my home office, with white plantation shutters on the windows and a gorgeous view of the mountains and the ocean beyond. My dogs were resting at my feet and I was writing at the computer.

One year later I was living in a city twenty-five miles north of where I had been previously, and in a brand new home with an office almost exactly as I had drawn it, even though I did not recognize this at that time. When I did, I went through everything on my shelves to finally locate that picture. It was uncanny when I saw the resemblance and detail to what I was now living.

When you are transforming at this rate of speed sometimes there is a time warp. It had been several months after I was living in my new home before I would make the connection between drawing the home office I wanted to manifest and sharing it with the others in my group and the fact that this was now my current reality. Talk about blowing your mind with the possibilities, and this was only the beginning!

You must have at least a simple vision of what it is you want to achieve as an entrepreneur. It may be based on a dream you have held in your mind and your heart for any number of years, or of a desired end result. Go for the thoughts you have had first, then the feelings, and on to the actions you believe necessary to put the wheels in motion.

Mine was a combination of these thoughts and feelings and actions, and it wasn't until the pain was so great from not being able to live a life I loved and feeling like my desired life was passing me by that I was ready to move forward with this vision.

Think about your life so far. Make a list of your accomplishments and your failures. Yes, I am using the "failure" word to describe everything you have ever attempted that did not work out because you failed to plan, to get started, to follow through, to ask for help, to do your best, to keep going when the going got tough, to course correct, and to see through to completion. Everyone fails, and successful entrepreneurs fail more often that the average person because we are determined to make things happen. Get into the habit of failing forward each time and discover what can transpire when you do.

In the twenty-first century entrepreneurs are described as "makers"; those who make or produce or create something. If you have ever thought of yourself as a creator, a poet, a builder, an inventor, a designer, a writer, or a creative, you are a maker. Makers work on multiple projects simultaneously.

It's Monday afternoon and I have made it from my house in Santa Clarita through the Mojave Desert, to Victorville, where I am used to getting on Interstate 15 to drive on to Las Vegas. Today I will continue on this highway only as far as Barstow where I will then take the exit for Interstate 40 East towards Needles, California. This is where I stop for lunch and to fill up my tank. The prices of gasoline are similar to what I pay in southern California, meaning that I'm still too close to home to see any lower prices. I remind myself to be patient.

It's not too hot and I am anxious to continue to where I will spend my first night in Flagstaff, Arizona. It's been almost three decades since I was there in my own car, and that was with my first husband and sometimes my now adult stepchildren. The sun is going down behind me and I look straight ahead as I enter the freeway once again.

# Getting Started

*Start before you're ready.*
~ Steven Pressfield

As I drive away from Flagstaff that next morning I see signs for Northern Arizona University, a college I knew nothing about until my friends back home announced their daughter had been accepted there for the 2016 fall semester. I gaze past the off ramp and decide I do not need to get off and take a photo of this school. But I will exit in an hour to spend some time in Winslow, the city mentioned in the 1972 Eagles song "Take It Easy." I passed up the comfort food being served at Cracker Barrel back in Flagstaff in favor of the ever so slightly healthier fare at an interesting local place called Joe and Aggie's Cafe along old Route 66 in Holbrook.

My past is getting further away with each mile marker. I grasp at thoughts and memories to bring my thinking around to where I want it to be as I continue to drive into the morning sun. My mind drifts back to the fall of 2005, a time when I was hungry for a new life.

At that time I had been a school teacher for nineteen years and no longer loved this career. Everything about it had changed since I had gone back to school at age 30 to earn my teaching credential during the late 1980s. I was exhausted physically, mentally, and psychologically from the experience and knew I would not easily make it to age sixty-eight when I could retire with a full pension and medical benefits.

The summer of 2005 had been an awakening for me. I had met some people who introduced me to the ideas around reinventing and designing my life in a way that made sense for where I was in my life at that time. I began reading books on a variety of topics that opened my mind to new possibilities. And

I was attending conferences and seminars every six weeks or so based on the program I mentioned in the first chapter.

But every day I looked in the mirror and asked myself the same question: How will I support myself and help out my elderly mother if I leave teaching and real estate? I prayed for an answer, a solution, even an idea. And that came in October of 2005 as I listened to a CD during my drive to school one morning.

I don't remember the man's name any longer because he seemed to evaporate from the internet soon after this time, but he was talking about setting up one page websites where he sold information on various topics.

One of these topics was wedding toasts, where the groom asks one of his friends or relatives to say a few words and to make a toast to the bride and groom at the reception, immediately following the wedding. As much as someone wants to do this for their close friend or family member, it isn't so easy to come up with something appropriate. Typically they are given short notice and find themselves getting bogged down with how they will be able to pull this off successfully.

The internet to the rescue, where you can search for anything and everything and come up with a solution quickly. The solution, in this case was an eBook containing a selection of wedding toasts, as well as some ideas and fill in the blank templates to come up with your own. It was a digital download, so you did not have to wait to receive the information. The cost was $27 and considered reasonable by the person who needed it right then.

He gave more examples on the CD about how he had set up a business he was running entirely from home on his personal computer. I became more and more excited at the possibilities and my world changed during my drive that morning.

Maybe I could do this. Perhaps I could learn how to come up with my own ideas and learn how to set up these simple websites. But it is 2005 and even though I have a computer at home and computers in my classroom and have even written grants to have more technology for the classroom and my students I have absolutely no idea about how to get started and what to do.

### The Moment of Decision

At recess I make a list of what I want to do. There are two columns; one of what I know how to do and the other one is for everything else. It's lopsided and I realize I need more information and guidance before I can truly begin.

In the column of things I know how to do is word processing and blogging. I had created a simple blog for my class to use during our science fair. We all learned together how to add images and text and to connect one post to another post or to a page.

Then one day I was clicking around on the blog and clicked to change the language from English to either French, German, or Spanish. I am fluent in Spanish and French has some similarity to Spanish because it is also a Latin based language, but on that day I choose German. Then I click around some more and end up clicking on a German phrase that translates to "delete this site forever." Live and learn.

But I was not to be deterred by this faux pas. No way would I allow a mistake of the past negatively affect my future.

Instead, I started another blog, and then another, and soon I was the proud own of a dozen blogs, created on free platforms and each about one of a dozen different topics ranging from walking for fitness to the law of attraction to writing eBooks. I told myself back then I was an educated woman with diverse interests and experiences and that I could not be limited to writing about a single topic.

That strategy did not serve me well. But the most important lesson I took away from those early days was the importance of getting started before you are ready and of taking consistent action. I learned so much from my mistakes, got over my fears and tendency towards perfectionism, and found people who would guide me to the success I so longed for in my life.

When you take action, you then have different questions. Think about that statement for a minute. Have you found this concept to be true? When I work with entrepreneurs many times it is around both tactics and strategies I have taught them and that they have not yet implemented. For example, one of my precepts is that blogging consistently is the way to create a body of work and build a platform simultaneously.

When I work with someone who wishes to become successful with online entrepreneurship I ask them about their blog and their content creation and publication strategy and plan. I can tell right away from their questions whether or not they have embraced and internalized this philosophy of writing to build their business.

The exit for Winslow, Arizona is just ahead. I plan to visit "Standin' on the Corner" park. It contains a two-story mural by John Pugh that appears to be three dimensional but is not, and a bronze statue by Ron Adamson of a life-sized man who is standing on a corner with a guitar by his side. The park is surrounded by a wall of bricks, each with a donor's name on it, and a story by each of the donors describing their fondness for this place. As soon as I experience this for myself I'm sure I will have different questions from the ones I have now. See how I did that?

# The Mentor

*The delicate balance of mentoring someone is not creating them in your own image, but giving them the opportunity to create themselves.*
~ Steven Spielberg

It's day three of my road trip and I'm headed east- northeast from Albuquerque, New Mexico to Oklahoma City and on to Tulsa, Oklahoma. I've been weaving on and off of what used to be historic Route 66 since leaving home. In years past I have driven all two thousand four hundred forty-eight miles of this road from Santa Monica, California to Chicago, Illinois and then back again, but this time that is not my focus. This part of the United States is flat and dusty and comforting in many ways, as in how it has changed so little over the years.

Other than my back being a little sore, most likely from the soft, sagging mattresses in the hotels I've stayed in for the past two nights, I am feeling good, thinking clearly and very appreciative for the good weather. I breathe in slowly and exhale deeply, in gratitude for the life I have created for myself. I want more, much more, if only for how this will allow me to help more people who come to me wanting to start their own journey of transformation.

So many of us live a life of mediocrity, wishing and hoping for more depth and breadth in our life experience, but not knowing how to achieve this goal. This I know from my own personal experiences. I felt so unfocused and alone for most of my adult life, until I made the conscious decision to leave teaching and real estate behind and start my own business I could run from home on the internet.

As I make my way each day, a lone traveler in the middle of the country I think back to my early days as an entrepreneur. I was alone then as well, finding my way in a new world where there were no road maps or a GPS navigation system to guide me. Even though I approached my new business with enthusiasm, soaking up every aspect of what was necessary in order to be successful, what I truly needed was a mentor.

I had begun to find people who proclaimed to be coaches and mentors to people like me, but who were not quite successful in their own right. For that and other reasons none seemed to be the right fit for me. They were all too aggressive or too wishy-washy or too aloof or too something for my taste. I did spend money with a couple of them; five thousand dollars from the money I had cashed out of my retirement fund as a teacher that I was living on while I built my business with one of them, only to find out none of these people would be willing or able to help someone as new to all of this as I was at that time.

And just as you may have said while you were growing up and believed your parents to be unfair on some issue, "when I grow up it will be different," I did the same. My exact words were more like "when I figure out how to become an online entrepreneur and begin earning steady income, I will reach out to the new people and teach them everything I know."

My search for the right mentor continued, and during 2007 I joined a program that came the closest to what I was looking for, and at a very fair price. It was a twelve week course on blogging taught by Patsi Krakoff and Denise Wakeman, known at that time as the "Blog Squad."

In the last chapter I wrote about the concept of asking different questions once you had taken action with something you wanted to learn and master. That was definitely the case when I went through their training. At the beginning I had so many questions about the basics of setting up and maintaining a blog, but due to the fact that I had not done this since leaving the classroom and starting my online business the year before my questions were almost pointless. It was Denise Wakeman who gently nudged and guided me to take action. She both inspired and motivated me and that got me moving forward.

My results were instantaneous and messy. Then I had questions based on what had actually occurred instead of what might happen hypothetically. Our group members learned from each other in the process and I was down to focusing on two blogs instead of a dozen. My actions were not based on blindly following a set of tactics, but on strategically doing what was working for me and based on what I was learning and implementing on an almost daily basis.

Having a mentor who not only had experience doing something I wanted to emulate but also specifically in the areas when I needed help and direction made all of the difference.

The following year I attended something called the "Big Seminar", hosted by Armand Morin. I had made a huge effort to get to Atlanta for this event, spending two thousand dollars on my seminar ticket, another three hundred for my airline ticket, and sharing a room with a woman I had met online to save some money there.

Armand provided lunch and dinner on each of the three days and it was during those meals, sitting elbow to elbow with some of the brightest and most innovative minds on the planet that I could see my future as the entrepreneur I so wanted to become. That is why I joined Armand's mentor program on the third day and why my belief in mentors continues to be a strong one. I stayed with Armand's group for six years, until I had outgrown it and needed to move on. We all continue to be friends and colleagues and are proud of each other's accomplishments.

Seek out mentors who can accelerate your learning and progress. Make sure you know who they are by getting on to their list, making small purchases (less than a hundred dollars) from them, and emailing them to make sure they will reply when you have a question. When you find someone who resonates with you and whom you feel will be able to help you, grab hold and don't let go. I am still in touch with all of the mentors who helped me, even those before I came online in 2006 and feel connected to them and acknowledge their role in my success. I also send my people to them when there are topics I am not experienced enough in to help them myself. And another thing: before choosing someone as a mentor, make sure they are still working with at least one mentor. We never get to the point where we can be without someone in our lives to be there for us in that way.

Tomorrow morning I will drive another four hundred miles along Interstate 44 to St. Louis, Missouri. I had hoped to make a stop in Springfield, Missouri to have lunch with a client who has taken several of my online courses, but I'm just not quite up to it. As I drive through her town I slow down a bit and imagine being able to spend time with her. I tell myself a true mentor would not be stopped by a little back pain. But the moment has passed and I speed up again on my way northeast. The three hours fly by and finally I see my exit.

In St. Louis I will spend a couple of days with Hans, my former exchange student, now in law school at George Washington University. Making the decision to take this road trip was an excellent idea.

Something is shifting in my mind and I can't put my finger on what it means. My past is getting further away with each mile marker.

# Section Two - The Road Map

*It is a rough road that leads to the heights of greatness.*
~ Lucius Annaeus Seneca

A road map is not a plan; far from it. It is an outline for the story you will live as you move from Point A to Point Z and all the points in between.

My path as an entrepreneur has been anything but linear and smooth. It has been jagged, dog-eared, bumpy, rumpled, and every other descriptor that can refer to situations that turn out so differently from what you intended.

My background and life experiences led me to pursuing perfection and stability in my life. I demanded to know the steps involved and to avoid the pitfalls of making bad, wrong, or incorrect decisions at every turn. The result? I was paralyzed by the fear that comes with not knowing which way to turn and which decision to make. In short, I believed that by not choosing I could avoid being wrong, when in fact, my lack of choice was always a wrong choice.

This thinking all came crashing down on me as I went through my life. At some point during the summer of 2005 I was willing to admit that out loud, at least while I was home alone and planning my next moves. Instead of a plan I created a road map of sorts for the journey on which I was about to embark.

I stood in front of my bathroom mirror and said,

"My name is Connie and I am a recovering perfectionist. Every day I will look for the times where I demand perfection from myself and those around me and I will ponder the choices I could make to move myself closer to my goals and dreams."

It is said that if you don't know where you're going, any road will take you there. In my quest for perfection I had placed my focus and emphasis on carefully making progress down the road, only to find that I was on the wrong road. Wrong for me. Incorrect for me. Uncomfortable for me. Not the right road for me and who I was as a human being. I needed desperately to get off that road and take a different path. At age fifty I politely excused myself from that road and skipped joyfully over to another one. The right one. The correct one. A comfortable one...for me.

So here I was on a very hot and humid June day in 2016, on an actual road trip where my plan for the perfect trip was coming to an end, not because of anything I had done wrong or incorrectly but due to the fact that life happens, and it can be messy as it unfolds. For it is only by experiencing situations that are almost completely out of our control that we may learn how to move forward in a way that serves us and our goals.

# Fuel Tank on Empty

*The moment you take responsibility for everything in your life is the moment you can change everything in your life.*
~ Hal Elrod

I pull up in front of the two story brick building that Hans has called home for a year now here in St. Louis. My back is worse and I have difficulty getting out of the car. I'm sure he lives upstairs and not sure if I can make it. I get out of the car carefully and attempt to stand up. No, this is too difficult. The pain shoots down my spine and through my left leg. What is this?

Leaning on the car door I fumble through my purse and dig out my phone. The last time we spoke was the night before I left home for this trip. Four days ago. Four very long days ago when I was not in this excruciating pain.

"Hans? Hi. Yes, downstairs. Please come down."

I look up to see him peering through the curtains and moments later he has bounded down the stairs and out to the street to greet me. He's a man now, twenty-three years old, a law student, and living on his own. There's a roommate, but he has gone home to China for the month and I will have his room during my intended two day visit. No, of course there is no elevator and yes, he has prepared some food for us.

I'm not sure how I make it up the stairs. The events of the next twenty-four hours are a blur. I do not want to burden my young friend with my situation.

Hans serves me a delicious homemade Chinese meal that he has spent time learning to prepare in the traditional manner. He wants to take me to see Gateway Arch National Park, but I have to decline his invitation because I'm just in too much pain. He tells me all about the place in vivid detail so I will at least be able to live the experience vicariously through him. The riverboat cruise gives you a different perspective. The tram ride tour takes you six hundred thirty feet to the top. The arch was designed by Finnish-America architect Eero Saarinen. Yes, it is fascinating. No, my extended family members in Finland have never mentioned this to me.

We stay up until two in the morning, catching up and sharing our latest life adventures. Neither of us mentions my back and leg pain and it becomes the elephant in the room. The following morning I discover I cannot get my leg high enough to get into the shower. I use a washcloth the best I can, get dressed, and wake up Hans to tell him I need to go to the closest urgent care facility. If I can get into my car I will go alone. Yes, I can do it. Yes, I promise to call him as soon as I know what's going on. I drive away slowly. My fuel tank is now on empty, but I have three quarters of a tank of gas in my car.

Life is messy. Business is as well. Accepting this as fact eliminates the need for perfectionism and impatience, but that doesn't mean you won't continue to want these both as a part of your life experience. Therein lies the dilemma for entrepreneurs. We want it fast and we want it to be perfect. We often say this as we are plowing through piles of papers looking for the one we need, searching by every word we can think of for that misfiled article in our Dropbox or email message in our Gmail account, and attempting to figure out how we missed this morning's dental appointment that we will now be charged for anyway.

This is the point where people I have mentored lament their plight; if they still had a job they would get regular paychecks, and paid medical, and sick days and vacation time. They would also have someone else shouldering the responsibility for the work that is done. I remind them why they are not at that job any longer. Soon they agree that it wasn't so wonderful after all.

The prescribed treatment for messiness, as it pertains to business is three fold. You must maintain focus, gain clarity, and persevere under any situations that may arise. Any one of these can be easily achieved, at least for short periods by almost anyone under any circumstances; succeeding with the trifecta I am presenting here is another story altogether. I will define each of these before going into greater detail as to how you can achieve them simultaneously and consistently

- Focus is the ability to block out everything in favor of one specific thing that you have taken on as a priority. Right now my focus is on writing this book.
- Clarity is the state of full confidence and belief in yourself, your ideas, your actions, and your goal. With clarity comes true vision and awakening.
- Perseverance is the unwavering commitment to your goal, despite difficulty or delay. Become steadfast in your determination and persistent in your efforts to find purposefulness in your actions.

The journey is our road trip to our destination. The target is ever changing as we learn and grow and interact. Keep your mind's eye on the goal, do not waver from your beliefs, and allow your goal to shift daily as you keep moving.

Think about your morning routine. Mine actually begins the afternoon or evening before, when I go through my "dynamic" to-do list to prioritize my tasks, activities, and goals for the following day. Then I make sure to get to bed early and arise the next morning at the time I know will work best for me in terms of being the most alert and focused and ready to begin my day. That time is four or four-thirty and I look forward to greeting my day when most of the world in my time zone is still asleep.

### Challenges and Responsibilities

Yes, life and business are messy, and you can keep that messiness at bay when you set yourself up for success and know how to face and address any challenges that come up for you. As Hal Elrod said in the quote at the beginning of this chapter, the moment you take responsibility for everything in your life is the moment you can change everything in your life.

It was in 2005 that I was first exposed to this idea of taking full responsibility for everything in my life. It sounded odd to me at first, as if it would be impossible for me to take responsibility for the weather, or someone else's behavior, or anything else completely out of my realm of control. But I soon learned that I was thinking about this in the wrong way. I took responsibility for this "wrong" thinking in order to move forward.

During my twenty years working as a classroom teacher while also running my real estate brokerage and appraisal business it was common for me to place blame for my circumstances and life experiences each day. The ever elusive "they" were responsible for problems I had with the people in my life, my happiness or lack thereof, and especially my financial situation.

If they hadn't raised property taxes and interest rates I could have sold more houses. If the appraisal industry hadn't changed the rules regarding new people coming in to the profession I could have increased my fees. If the school district had given the teachers the choice in which math and reading programs we would use in the classroom, the students would have scored higher on the state tests.

In the aforementioned examples, I was placing the blame on governmental entities and regulatory committees. It was easy to blame people I had not met for messing up my life. If they knew me they would understand why I was being negatively affected by their decisions.

Then there was the blaming of people I did know, both personally and in my career and business. The principal wasn't fair to me because the other teacher is her friend. My neighbor doesn't care that Sunday morning is the only time I can get an extra hour of sleep so he uses his hedge clippers and wakes me up. My friend cancelled our lunch date because she had something else she preferred to do at that time.

I could go on and on but I think you get the point. It was always someone else's fault and almost never something I could have been responsible for to have a different outcome.

My "wrong" thinking was exposed on a warm spring evening in early May of 2005 when I attended a seminar with a friend. Actually, my friend had invited me but then made an excuse as to why she couldn't come and I decided to go by myself. I can't recall the exact name of this event but it was something around changing your thinking to increase your income. I was ready to do this because I had set as my goal to learn how to change the people around me so I could earn more money in my real estate business. Did you get that? I wanted to *change other people* in order to achieve my financial goals. At that time I honestly believed this was possible.

The seminar was being held at a hotel I had only been to a couple of times before, and not recently. There were several speakers and the first one was a woman who appeared to be in her early fifties. She was dressed nicely and her voice was soft yet authoritative. I liked her right away and smiled back when she made eye contact with me. I was sitting in the front row with my notebook open and ready so I could take notes.

You can imagine my shock when she called on me to stand up and answer a question. Instantly my admiration for her changed to slight dislike. Why would she put me on the spot like this? I wanted to leave but so many people were now arriving it would have been awkward to attempt an escape from the room.

I took a deep breath and let it out slowly. She took a step forward and asked,

"Did you have any difficulty finding the hotel this evening?"

I could answer that question. It was an easy one.

"No, I knew exactly where it was located."

"How is the parking?"

I knew this one too.

"The last time I was here they had a parking lot on the side. But now you have to go into the parking structure."

"So you were able to park easily?"

I started to feel uncomfortable. Where was she going with this line of questioning?

"I wouldn't say it was easy. I wasn't sure which room we were meeting in and I went in the wrong entrance. The parking attendant wouldn't let me turn around and go out and then in again at the proper entrance. He forgot to give me my ticket and then I had to find my way in to the hotel and figure out which floor we would be on. The lady at the information counter sent me to the right floor but to the wrong room."

The speaker paused and looked out at the audience before looking back at me.

"Is there anything else you'd like to add?"

"I got here in time and that's why I'm in the front row. Five more minutes and that would not have been the case. And there was more traffic than I had anticipated, but I made it in time."

She thanked me, the people in the room gave me a polite round of applause, and I had never been so happy to sit down. It felt like everyone was staring at the back of my head so I didn't dare turn around.

Over the course of the next two hours my answers to those seemingly innocent, simple, and straightforward questions were used as examples of how to change our thinking to increase our income, the topic of the seminar. I learned that by taking full responsibility for every situation you take back your power and have a choice in the outcome.

It turned out more than half of the people in the room had experienced what I had in driving to the hotel, parking, and finding our meeting room. Another forty percent had gone through something very unpleasant due to not being able to leave work in time, having family members who needed them to help with one thing or another, or not knowing where the hotel was located and getting caught in rush hour traffic. I found myself judging them for not being more organized.

Then there was the final five or so percent of those in attendance that evening. These people identified themselves and raised their hands when another speaker asked who had a joyous or funny or empowering story to share about coming to the hotel and making their way to our room.

After listening to two of these people tell their story I was sure they had been planted in the audience by the event organizers. They absolutely gushed when telling of deciding to drive with a friend or taking public transportation, and of calling the hotel earlier in the day and asking specific questions in advance so they would be prepared. One woman had even spoken to someone in housekeeping to find out what temperature the room would be at this evening. She held up a delicate white sweater with gray beads along the sleeves and proclaimed "This is my event sweater - it goes with everything I own!" to which she received a hearty cheer and a vigorous round of applause.

I didn't feel so good but I knew this was information I needed to hear. The final speaker for the evening was a man who had been trained as an engineer but had changed careers and now worked in sales and as a life coach. Life coaching was a new concept to me at that time and he explained what it meant to him and to the people he worked with.

He talked about taking full responsibility for our life experience in order to achieve our goals. I was afraid he might call on me but instead he asked a man sitting further back in the room to please stand up. This man was one who had a similar experience to what I'd had earlier in the evening. He was asked what he might do differently if he had this day to live over again. He answered,

"I'd be better prepared. I would have asked someone to come with me tonight and arranged that a week ago. We could have parked at the Metro Link station and taken the train to this stop, just a block from this hotel. I would have called the hotel yesterday to find out exactly where we would be meeting. And I would have looked up any restaurants or coffee shops nearby so my friend and I could have sat down to enjoy each other's company for a half hour before coming in to the hotel."

And then he said something that brought about a shift in my thinking.

"I can now see that taking responsibility frees me from blaming others. It feels good to make sure you have done what you can to ensure a more positive outcome."

As the event ended and we filed out the doors, a feeling of pride and empowerment washed over me. Feeling like my fuel tank was on empty was a choice I was making each day. From now on my goal was to live each moment as though I had a full tank and was ready to face the world in a positive and uplifting way.

# Which Path Makes Sense?

*You cannot change your destination overnight,*
*but you can change your direction overnight.*
~ Jim Rohn

The Urgent Care is four exits down the freeway and takes me across the Mississippi River and into east St. Louis. Driving is the most comfortable position for me today, but getting in and out of the car can be problematic. Using my GPS I easily find the location. It's in a strip mall right off the freeway and I pull in to a spot close to the entrance.

They sit me down in a wheelchair and push me up to the counter. I provide my driver's license and insurance card and they ask for a credit card because I'm from out of state and my insurance may not cover this visit.

I am wheeled into a little room where a doctor shows up quickly. Two minutes later she tells me I must go to the hospital's emergency room because this is too serious for them to handle.

Back in the car. Buckled in. Wincing at the pain. Another three exits and I am there. I'm in East St. Louis now and it looks very different from Hans' neighborhood five miles away. I need to call him. I'll wait until the ER people tell me what they think. There is no parking directly in front of the hospital's emergency room so I find the parking lot. The sun is pounding down on me as I carefully exit my vehicle. I'm out of the car, I have my purse and keys, and it's so very hot.

The last thing I see is the sun in my eyes. I'm going down and there is no sound. There is no pain. I feel nothing and it is peaceful. There is no sun now, only darkness and quiet and no pain. Thank you, Lord, I can't take any more of this pain.

Now someone is lifting me effortlessly into a chair, it must be a wheelchair. I want thank them but they have no face and I have no voice. I'm floating past images that are either cars or trees or both. The quiet feels good. Please, let me stay here awhile to catch my breath and get some rest. I'm just so tired.

It's noisy now, and cold. I look up into the eyes of a young African-American boy who can't be more than three years old. He's in my personal space but I don't care. I smile and he says "hi" and looks down. I wait for him to make eye contact again and I tell him my name. He runs back into his mother's waiting arms.

I say my name again and I'm being wheeled into the emergency room. X-rays followed by an MRI and then an EKG and I'm wondering how much this will all cost. Then I remember that I have insurance and then I remember I am in Missouri and it may not, will probably not be covered. I don't care. I am grateful for this help and care they are providing for me. I can't remember the name of this hospital that is so clean and feels very safe. I exhale, slowly, feeling every space in my rib cage and diaphragm opening up and closing again around my breaths.

Now I'm lying down on one of those beds that are always too small behind a flimsy curtain. The doctor and his team come in and surround me, forming a perfect semi-circle as if they have performed this scene many times before in the medical theatre of the absurd. I am feeling no pain and say something to them I intend to be funny. No one laughs.

The leader of this pack speaks directly to me and all eyes are on him. He is the orthopedist who examined me earlier and ordered tests I now cannot fully remember.

"You have injured your back and have a condition called sciatica. This was exacerbated by your drive over the past three days. You must fly back to California immediately and make arrangements for your car."

All eyes shift to me, in unison as if being orchestrated by a special effects team. I think about responding to his comment. It didn't seem like I had been in the car too long each day. I've driven across the country many times, but that was decades ago. I don't want to turn back now. If I am going to be in pain anyway, why not continue my trip.

"How long before the morphine wears off?" I ask.

"Morphine has a short half-life. In a couple of hours it will be out of your system completely."

A beat. Whoever speaks next will have the power.

"Please give me a prescription and thank you, thanks to all of you for taking care of me."

I look around the circle and attempt to make eye contact with as many of these dedicated medical workers as possible. They each look identical to me in my drugged state.

The doctor lingers for a moment, looking deeply into my eyes, knowing I will not be returning to California that day or the next. He clears his throat, his entourage shifts their body position in unison and they all leave from the direction they came, the flimsy gray curtain whooshing in the breeze of their motions.

Minutes later I am dressed and being wheeled out the door to the parking lot.

"Good luck to you," says the orderly as he assists me out of the wheelchair. The half-life still has a little life and I'm pain free getting into my car.

Over the next several hours I drive on Interstate 55 into Illinois, zigzagging down through Arkansas and over to Paducah, Kentucky because I missed an exit, and finally into Tennessee, only stopping once to use the restroom and to fill up with gas. The prices are lower here and it seems like a million years since I first thought about that back in Arizona.

In Memphis, Tennessee I find a drive-through pharmacy to get my prescriptions filled. There is enough for three days and I quickly do the math to figure out how to make it last until I get home seventeen days from now. The numbers don't look good, but I have chosen my path and my direction.

I have only looked at my maps once during this trip. Before I left I went in to the AAA office in Santa Barbara and asked them for detailed maps of each section of the United States I would be driving through, as well as something they still call a "Trip-Tik", which takes you mile by mile through your drive, pointing out landmarks and places of interest and informing you of the speed limits and road laws that differ from state to state in our country.

Instead, I choose to use my navigation system in my Honda Pilot to chart my course each day. I do not need to know how to get from my home in southern California to my client's home in Bowie, Maryland (my furthest point east) in order to make this trip; I only need to know how to drive from where I am at this moment to the location I have chosen to reach a few hours from now to rest for the night. This is the same for our businesses and I will share my thoughts on that topic with you here...

No matter what you goal in life, you do not need to know the details of how you will get there from where you are right now. In fact, it is far wiser to think of this goal as being a moving target, one in which you only want to be three steps ahead at any time. Because once you get closer to this goal you will need to step back and course correct in order for it to continue to be a viable goal for you and the lifestyle you are designing for yourself. This leads to inner game mind shifts that can either serve to catapult you forward to the great success you want and deserve or to hold you back until you decide to give up.

At some point every entrepreneur reaches a point where they get stuck and must make a choice as to the direction they want to take their business. I'm not talking about the choices you make when you are first starting out; no, I am referring to the day when you take a look at what you are doing and the results you are getting and think that maybe it has all been wasted time. We've all been there.

Looking back, I'm not sure what I was thinking when I made the decision in the late fall of 2005 to leave my teaching position at the end of that school year and to give my best real estate clients away to those who could better serve them by the end of June, 2006. I had no real plan and did not know how I would earn any income. But I was filled with hope and strong on faith and made the jump anyway.

That first month I decided to help people who wanted to write and sell eBooks, based upon my experience with editing my student's writing for twenty years and helping adult friends with their various writing projects over many years. I wasn't a writer but had lots of experience editing. The marketing was new to me and I just figured my new clients and I would all learn together.

It was a year and a half later that I reached the point in my own business I am talking about here. I could have continued to mentor people through the process of choosing a niche and a topic, writing their eBook, publishing it and finally marketing it. I was earning money doing this and had even published my own eBook on the topic of real estate farming. It was doing well and served as an excellent example of how to succeed with this business model from start to finish. But I wanted more. I wanted a lot more.

So I was at a crossroads and had to choose my path and my direction. I had already learned how to make money online, and in fact had replaced my previous income as a teacher and working part-time in real estate. My goal now was to make a name for myself that I could be proud of and to help more people achieve their goals as online entrepreneurs.

The next leg of my journey would be to conquer the world of internet marketing. Few women were in this space at that time, and that was another reason I wanted to break in. One person takes the leap without falling into a dark crevice and many others will follow. This felt like something I wanted and needed to do. I was a pioneer woman, albeit in a digital world with electricity, the internet, and other conveniences.

The only thing that stops any of us is our own thinking and belief system. These are known as limiting beliefs. I knew very little about this area of life when I came online. Now it is the main focus of my own study and what I share with my community online and offline. I will not share the clichés you have heard so many times. Instead, I will share with you by example how this continues to work for me.

I believed that I could not be a writer. That was not true at all. It only became my belief because I so seldom wrote anything and when I did I rarely shared it with others. I think back to the job I had at a production company years ago where I approached J. Michael Straczynski with my story idea. He is a prolific writer and is best known as the creator of the science fiction television series *Babylon 5*. He has been described as being one of the greatest science fiction minds of all time. Back in 1985 when I knew him he was a staff writer for an animated television series called *Jayce and the Wheeled Warriors*. He is kind but firm when he tells me, "Don't tell me your story. Write your story and I will read it." I was not brave enough to follow through with this advice and regret it to this day.

Once I began writing I was a writer. The very definition of a writer is "one who writes." This book contains the one million, six hundred thousandth word I have written and published and you read right past it a chapter or so back.

Also, I believed I could not become a public speaker. This was based on my fear of speaking in front of adults anywhere, except in a group of three or four people. Then I joined Rotary, an international service organization and they began passing the microphone to me almost every week so I could share the projects our club was working on, in the community and around the world.

Once I spoke to an audience I became a speaker. Soon I was speaking at the district level and the following year I was asked to speak at a marketing event in Atlanta. This year I am hosting my twenty-fourth live event and speak at many other conferences, retreats, and seminars on the topics of authorship, mindset shifts, and entrepreneurship all over the world.

If you can think about the concept you want to achieve, you can take the necessary action steps to make it happen. Everything we do moves us closer to or further away from our goals. If I had chosen to return to California at the doctor's recommendation back in St. Louis I would have been taking myself further away from my goal of completing my seventeen state, six thousand three hundred mile road trip, where I spent meaningful, joyous, productive time with more than a dozen clients, students, friends, and family members. The day I spent in the emergency room was my crossroads and I had just a split second in time to choose my path, commit to the direction, and go for my goal. Most likely you will always have more time than that to make your decision, but do it as quickly as possible and leap into the next chapter of your journey.

My next stop will be in Memphis, a city I have driven through several times as a younger person and one that I look forward to seeing once again. Long ago I visited a recording studio there and saw Elvis Presley's microphone. It made me teary eyed for some reason, even though I was never an Elvis fan. Nostalgia can be funny that way.

# Section Three - The Detour

*A truly happy person is the one who can enjoy the scenery while on a detour.*
~ Unknown

When you start out as an entrepreneur you believe that you must learn everything there is to know before you can begin. This becomes an endless chase for the carrot at the end of the stick as you spin 'round and 'round on the hamster wheel of business. Perhaps you have experienced this yourself.

But soon you will discover this frenzied pace can only be maintained for a short period of time. Then you either jump off or fall off, exhausted by the whirlwind of activity that has consumed you for some brief period of time and taken you to the extremes of positive and negative emotions, feelings of confidence and self-doubt, and thoughts of potential success and of personal and professional failure. This isn't healthy and certainly not productive.

Now you're ready for a detour of sorts. You know there must be a better way to earn income and work fewer hours as your own boss. I will give you a spoiler alert her and tell you there most definitely is a better and more rewarding way to approach entrepreneurship. You think back to the promises of time and financial freedom and wonder where you went wrong or at least took a misstep.

Perhaps you have dabbled as an entrepreneur. Maybe you experimented with two or three different niche topics and business models. This can be valuable or dangerous depending upon how you went about it and if you had a mentor guiding you in a way that allowed you to experience success on your terms.

I've recently been working with a man who has been online for about five years and has just made the wise decision to join my mentor program. I am not using the adjective *wise* in an arrogant manner at all; he has spent at least fifty thousand dollars during these years and has earned less than five hundred dollars as a result.

Choosing a "core" business to commit to will allow you to move quickly. Your detour will then be to explore all aspects of your business and see where you need to make some changes. My recommendation is to create a list, or a three circle Venn diagram to write down your responses to three items:

- Your passions, interests, things you love to do and be a part of in your life
- Your experiences, education, jobs, training, and everything you have had in front of you whether it was by choice or by chance
- The marketplace, where people are spending their time and money for products, courses, services, and coaching

You are looking for what we refer to as the "sweet spot"; that place where the three circles of your Venn diagram come together or where your lists merge. Your goal: to find a specific area that you feel strongly about, where you have some experience or training, and where the market is anxious to learn more and to pay for it. Once you find this place you will want to walk, run, skip, gallop, hop, and side-slide over to it immediately and give it all you've got.

I chose the niche of eBook writing, publishing and marketing to begin with. It fit my Venn diagram to a T based on my love of writing and my experience as a classroom teacher and allowed me to experience some success before I moved on a year and a half later to the broader niche of online marketing.

Affiliate marketing was my focus as a business model during that time. The first year I did not have any products of my own and instead preferred to recommend and promote products, courses, and services created by others. I only recommended what I used personally and was benefitting from so this was quite an effective model for me to pursue.

A year later I had my first product and it was soon followed by another, but affiliate marketing remained my primary source of income during that period of time.

My next detour was to market for local, small business owners and to add more products to my digital inventory. This took me to over a hundred thousand dollars a year in revenue and I knew at that time I could not only maintain this but also increase it steadily over time. A detour, or what can be referred to here as a "lateral arabesque" can lead to excellent results over time.

# A New Normal

*The desire to create is one of the deepest yearnings of the human soul.*
~ Dieter F. Uchtdorf

Memphis is bustling but not overcrowded, and filled with southern charm and personality. I've called ahead to ask for an "accessible" room at the motel where I will stay tonight. The man at the front desk is very kind and offers to bring my bags into the room. I accept his offer and find myself crawling into the bed as soon as he closes the door behind him, even though it is only about seven o'clock and still daylight outside.

This is the first time I will allow myself to cry after thinking about my predicament. I am two thousand miles from home and not able to walk without using a cane (at the last minute I had thrown the cane I had used several years ago after knee surgery into the car - not sure why but so thankful I did) and enduring incredible pain. This too will pass, I tell myself but I certainly wish I had a magic wand to wave to alleviate my pain and move forward more quickly. I wonder how long it will take to get back to my previous physical condition.

Memphis was one of the hubs for Northwest airlines years ago, before they merged with Delta in 2008 and closed this hub in 2013, so I've been to the airport here many times. I'm glad it's not raining and realize I still haven't yet come across any inclement weather after almost a week on the road. Has it only been six days so far since I drove away from California?

I am living a double life right now. Life inside of my car is tolerable because sitting in my seat allows me to feel like a human being with only minimal pain. The other half of my life consists of entering and exiting my car and walking slowly, each step more difficult than the one before, filling my tank with gasoline, going into stores and restaurants, and going in to motels to attempt to get some sleep, shower, and get dressed for the following day. Tomorrow I will be staying at the home of two of my clients and I am hoping and praying that will be more comfortable.

This pain is greater than anything I have ever experienced and I've been through a lot in my lifetime. This may be my new "normal" and I'm not ready to accept that.

Starting your business will require you to adopt a new "normal", at least during the first year or so. For me, that meant getting up in the morning at the same time as when I was teaching school and working in real estate after school and on the weekends, but doing it all from home with this online business. At first I created a work space in my bedroom, so I spent time in that room for as much as sixteen hours each day.

Over time I made some adjustments, like moving my bedroom and office into the master suite in my new house. There is a very large balcony off that room that allows me to step outdoors for periods of time to think, reflect, and sometimes to even do some work on my tablet or laptop when the weather is optimal and the sun is in just the right position in the sky.

The goal, perhaps is to morph your situation into a new normal that works for you.

I'm back in the car, satisfied with the amount of work I have been able to accomplish during the past twenty-four hours, well rested, and keeping the pain at bay. My new normal has me swinging my right leg up into the car and pulling the rest of me along as quickly afterward as possible. I'm sure it looks funny to onlookers, the pain makes me grimace, and I am just happy to be alive and enjoying my road trip. My vehicle is my stallion and I gallop down the road on my way to Nashville.

I find a country station on my satellite radio and sing along to Blake Shelton's latest hit, "Came Here to Forget." I heard him interviewed on the radio the day before and he is in the process of finding his new normal after his change in circumstances with the recent divorce from singer Miranda Lambert. He did not write this song but chose to record it for his album "If I'm Honest."

"I've had a lot of music over the years but I don't think I've ever had a song before that's such a direct look into my life," said Shelton "That's why I'm so excited about this particular song."

I sing along at the top of my lungs, channeling my inner rock star, albeit a country song.

*You better keep on keeping it lit*

*'Til we can't remember*

*Can't remember what we came here to forget*

Am I trying to forget something while I'm driving across the United States and back this month? I don't think so. I don't know. Already I am learning things about myself I did not know, like my threshold for pain and how grateful I am for every little thing I have. Self-discovery is a valuable process.

This song was recorded and produced in Nashville, the city I'll be sliding into later today.

# In Search of Boring

*Boredom is only for people with no imagination.*
~ Tim Tharp

Nashville is the city of dreams for people who love music, history, and culture. Even though country music dominates the music scene you will find every genre imaginable in this town. This is home to the Grand Ole Opry House stage, which is the world's longest running live radio show, and the Country Music Hall of Fame and Museum.

The Parthenon in Centennial Park is a full-scale replica of the original Parthenon in Athens, Greece. Another interesting fact is that the cholera outbreak that struck here in 1849/50 took the life of former U.S. President James K. Polk. My original plan had included getting out and seeing the sights but that isn't going to happen now.

Instead, I've checked into my motel room, powered up my laptop, and will eat the remainder of my lunch from Cracker Barrel for dinner while getting some work done. Boring, yes, but I enjoy my work and know I need to rest for twelve hours before hitting the road again by six or seven in the morning.

## Boring as a Lifestyle

The word and concept of "boring" has flowed in and out of my life for more than five decades now. As a kid I complained that I was bored when there was nothing to do and nowhere to go. My mother successfully combated this by taking me to the public library, the zoo, and to an occasional movie. Then she instructed me to read, draw pictures and write stories about the animals I had seen, or to act out a scene from the movie. In other words, she encouraged me to take each experience and build on it in a creative way.

As an adult I would get bored in settings that did not light me up. What I mean by this is that I preferred to be entertained than to buckle down to work. The work was boring. I craved ongoing cycles of excitement from outside people and events, followed by periods of silence and retreat into my own mind and personal space. I'm an introvert and can only handle just so much excitement, bright lights, and noise before I shut down and must escape into the quiet solitude.

As an entrepreneur I learned quickly that highs and lows are not ideal and that slow, steady growth is best. I figured out early on that craving and insisting on excitement can be dangerous and hamper your success for the long term.

## Let's Define Boring

The dictionary definition of this word is not interesting; tedious. Example: "I've got a boring job in an office."

Synonyms include: monotonous, repetitive, unrelieved, dull, tedious, unvaried, lifeless, unimaginative, uneventful; characterless, featureless, colorless, bland, insipid, flat, uninteresting, trying, unexciting, uninspiring, unstimulating, uninvolving; unreadable, unwatchable; jejune, dry, stale, tired, banal, lackluster, stodgy, vapid, monochrome, dreary, humdrum, mundane; mind-numbing, wearisome, tiring, tiresome, irksome, frustrating; deadly, ho-hum, dullsville, dull as dishwater, and plain-vanilla.

As I read these words I salivate in anticipation of what is possible. My boring business excites me in a way that wakes me up at 3 am with new ideas; brings out creativity in me that has helped me to change many hundreds of people's lives, and allows me to live a life that is filled with joy and freedom, and prosperity. I am literally being "bored to life" in every moment of every day.

The antithesis of boredom is engaging, exhilarating, breathtaking, and electrifying. It's up to you to reframe your business, and your life in this way.

You may be aware that many online entrepreneurs spend weeks or months leading up to a product launch, earn substantial income throughout their launch, and then retreat into oblivion for the remainder of the year. This strategy can be tricky and typically will bring in less revenue than that earned by someone who has structured their business is such a way as to have ongoing, flowing waves of income year around. This is similar to what my actor friends experience when they work intently on a play or a film for months on end and then have even longer periods of a dry spell where there is not a situation they feel strongly enough about to engage in and become committed to. Many choose work on television instead, because it is more conducive to family life and more predictable in terms of a schedule.

The latter, having a steady flow of work and income year round is my model and I can tell you two things about it; it allows me to add revenue and income every single month and it is pretty boring for the most part.

Being willing to be boring means doing the work and focusing on the one single thing that works for you. Show me an entrepreneur who cherishes the boredom of the daily work flow and I'll show you someone who is blissfully successful. You can still have some highs and lows within your business, such as when you launch a new product, course, live event, or book, but for the most part every day will have more similarities than differences.

Learning to love the work can be exhilarating in its own right. There is nothing at all boring about the four things I do every day in my business - writing, creating, marketing, and mentoring. I do each of these during my early morning "prime time" hours, when I am most alert and ready to engage in my tasks and activities. Earlier I shared more about the importance of having a daily routine and this is the part that makes me feel alive.

# Finding the Rhythm

*Every disciplined effort has its own multiple rewards.*
~ Matthew Kelly

I'm up at dawn, showered and ready for my new day. I had a banana and some yogurt first thing this morning. I was able to pick this up at the convenience store next to where I filled up with gasoline last evening.

As I drive east on Interstate 40 through Nashville I spot the exits for all the places I had intended to visit today. Instead of allowing this to get me down I promise myself that I will return and see even more sights in the near future.

My next stop is in Knoxville where I will have lunch with a colleague and then on to the tri-cities of Kingsport, Johnson City, and Bristol and the where I will stay with some family members and connect with several other family, two long time friends, and a brand new client. I'm still hoping for some rainfall to appear so perhaps this is the day.

My pain is minimal today and for that I am grateful.

In the last chapter I shared and explained why building a business in a slow and steady way makes more sense than one with extreme highs and the lows that come with that. This can be thought of as being quite boring, but I also shared how you can reframe that thinking and reap the psychological and financial benefits over time.

Leaving my position as a classroom teacher, giving away my best real estate clients, and making the transition to entrepreneurship was a bumpy road for me. Real estate was up and down depending upon so many factors outside of my control, so moving away from this career felt like the right thing for me to make at the time. And even though I did not wish to remain as an employee of the school district after serving for twenty years, there was a certain comfort in the paycheck, the medical coverage, and the almost predictable rhythm of each day. So as I began to set up my own business from first my bedroom and soon after my home office I decided to replicate that rhythm the best I could.

Each morning I got up at the same time I had previously, which is about five. I already had a list of things I wanted to accomplish that day. This came from what I continue to call my "dynamic to-do list" where anything not completed the day before simply rolls over to the next day, along with that day's tasks and activities. If something is not done by the third day I either take it off the list for good or delegate it to the person who is better equipped to do that task for me. My ongoing goal is to further perfect this process so that my business will run like clockwork.

Then I dig in and begin working, focusing on the four areas I mentioned in the last chapter - writing, creating, marketing, and mentoring. I do prioritize these and I will explain my process.

For example, I must write first thing in the morning while my thoughts and ideas are rushing towards the front of my mind. As I write this paragraph it is just after six in the morning. I outlined this part of the book last night before going to sleep so that it would come alive in my subconscious and be ready to be delivered to the page first thing this morning. If I'm not writing a book I am writing articles, blog posts, short reports, and emails to my community.

Creating refers to the products and courses I produce on a regular basis. Today, for example I will complete the rewrite for my ongoing training called "Affiliate Contest Secrets" and prepare for tomorrow's session for my "Really Simple Authority Blogging" online course. I will also do some work on a new product I am creating for authors called "Book Launch Booster Rockets" that will be released in the next month.

Marketing refers to the income producing activities I engage in every day. This includes writing and sending out an email that I have written earlier in the morning, publishing and syndicating articles and blog posts, sharing information on my products through my email message, short reports, and on social media, and connecting with colleagues regarding the promotion of their products or mine.

Mentoring is where I spend one-on-one time with the people who have chosen to work closely with me to build and grow their businesses. The flip side of this is the time I spend speaking with my own mentors to further my own business.

I am able to write about all of this so smoothly because I have created a natural rhythm around each piece. It is boring in that it is somewhat repetitive and predictable but I view it as the opportunity to keep my feet on the ground while my mind soars high in the clouds.

My results speak for themselves as I have created my own empire since beginning my business in 2006. If I had insisted on creating a business with highs and lows, annual or semi-annual product launches followed by periods of low or no sales, and a chaotic daily practice of chasing every bright shiny object that came my way, my results would be quite different. I shudder to think that I may not have been able to stay in business for all of these years.

Find your rhythm in every aspect of your life and business and see how that feels. Reframe your work life to where you look forward to following your own dynamic to-do list each day, crossing off the tasks and activities as they are completed and handing over those you will delegate to others who are better suited to work on those pieces of your business. An example of this is when I finally let go of attempting to create my own graphics. It was messing up my flow and rhythm but took me a couple of years to accept this was not an area of strength for me. Now outsourcing that task is a seamless piece of my business and I am back to only doing what I do best and enjoy doing each and every day.

Know and believe that you can change your life by changing your rhythm. I do not say this lightly but from my own experience and that of the people I work closely with. Develop a morning routine that serves you as the starting point for the direction you wish to go in.

Track your numbers, using the accomplishments and completions you achieve as your guide and then adding in the revenue and expenses associated with each one. This works, and works well if you adhere to a practice that you have set up for yourself. Far too many entrepreneurs and small business owners engage in random acts of busyness that do not lead to the results they were hoping for. Set your goals a bit higher than what you honestly believe you can achieve and then stretch yourself and do the work to get there.

Your life and business are a road trip in and of themselves. Create and live the journey that best suits you and your lifestyle will grow and prosper. Find your rhythm and sway to the music.

# Meet the Cousins

*Call it a clan, call it a network, call it a tribe, call it a family: Whatever you call it, whoever you are, you need one.*
~ Jane Howard

I pull into Kingsport just before eleven on this sunny morning in June and decide to make the rounds to all the places I know before heading to my aunt and uncle's home just outside of town. Nothing has changed much since I was here three years ago and I find that comforting in some ways. I park outside the mall but my back and legs are sore and I decide at the last minute to not go inside. I watch instead as shoppers enter and leave and imagine what they might have in the brightly decorated plastic and paper bags they are carrying.

My family members in Kingsport and Johnson City, Tennessee have gathered at the home of my aunt and uncle and are clearly excited to see me when I pull up in front of their house. They are from my mother's side of the family and relocated here when I was a teenager. Over the decades I have made every effort to see them every few years and these days they also come to see me in California or in various locations where I am speaking or attending an event. There is a new baby this time, my great nephew Caleb and I plan to take lots of photos of him and with him and the others.

They are shocked but not surprised when they see how difficult it is for me to get down and out of my car and I don't pretend it is nothing. They think of me as the one from California who is willing to try most anything.

My aunt was a second mother to me growing up and would be hurt if I didn't let her fuss over me about this. She calls out to my uncle to bring the "comfy" chair into the living room and my nephew, now a father for the first time takes my arm and helps me up the three big stairs to the front porch and then inside. When did he become such a mature man?

The comfy chair is just that and I sink down into the soft seat cushion. I breathe out a sigh of relief that I have finally made it to see the people that I have been most looking forward to spending some time with on this trip. All eyes are on me and I feel the need to speak first as everyone gathers around.

"It's so good to see everyone," I say, making eye contact from right to left and back again. "And that Caleb is a handsome little fellow."

This sets the stage for what becomes the highlight of my road trip for personal reasons. We stay up late, or late for me anyway talking and laughing and reminiscing and making new memories that will shine long after I have moved on to my next destination.

I had planned to create a new product and do all kinds of work while on my road trip. My goal was to spend two hours working each morning, and then another two in the evening before I went to bed. This did not pan out as my life turned into one of survival during these three weeks of intense travel and unbelievable pain.

My "new normal" backup plan came together as I was eating dinner in my motel room in Memphis two days earlier. If I could not spend a total of four hours a day working in my business, which was probably way too adventurous anyway while I was on the road, how could I maintain my level of income for three weeks?

I am a "maker" in the purest sense of that term; a writer, an idea person, a big thinker, a product creator, and a mentor. I have gone from thinking of myself as more of a logical, left-brained human to accepting and embracing the fact that I am a very creative person. This means that over the past decade I have written many books and created even more information products and courses that are already available for sale online.

These are accessible in digital formats, electrons just waiting to be downloaded and devoured by my hungry community of newer entrepreneurs.

That night, after baby Caleb was fast asleep and I had heard every story in great detail from eight extended family members, friends, and neighbors I powered up my laptop and got to work.

I went through five of my most popular online courses, updating where necessary and checking the membership areas and sales pages to make sure everything was correct and timely. Then I logged in to my author's account on Amazon and looked over my books, choosing five of them that I could offer for free in digital (Kindle) format for up to five days each as a part of their "Kindle Select" program.

All I needed to do now was to email my list each morning, something I do anyway and let them know which book was available at no cost and which online course was on sale for up to fifty percent off the regular price for the next three days. I also included an affiliate offer or two that helped spread the word for the awesome and talented people and their products I highly recommend.

This worked extremely well and allowed me to spend only about thirty minutes each day on the computer until I returned home. And the interesting thing was that I earned about fifteen percent more income during this period of time than I would have doing things the way I had planned. So this shift in strategy and energy paid off handsomely and I learned some things about my business I might not have figured out any other way, all while taking care of myself and my current predicament. Always look for the upside to a situation that seems doomed or impossible and I can guarantee you will stretch your thinking to make it happen in a positive way that is beneficial to everyone involved.

And as for that product I had intended to create while on my road trip? It got finished a month after I returned home and turned out very differently from how I had imagined it at the beginning of my trip. This is one of my favorite parts of entrepreneurship; the twists and turns that make what we engage in and create unique and special, and greatly influenced by our daily lives.

You are a creative person, even if you do not currently think of yourself in this way. You are also a problem solver. And my guess is that you also enjoy helping people to achieve their goals while sharing your special gifts and talents. When you combine the traits and qualities of someone who is a creative, problem solving person who also wants to help others you have the perfect storm for entrepreneurial success. I'll share a story and see if you can relate to it.

Back in 2006 when I was a brand new online entrepreneur I did not think of myself as being a creative person or much of a problem solver. But I did know that helping others was important in my life. So when my neighbor came to my door in tears I invited her in right away to see how I could help.

She was a real estate agent and we had met while our homes were being built in our new development. There were only a dozen houses going up in our area and many of us had become fast friends. On that day she told me that her husband had just told her she had to get a "real" job because she wasn't earning much in real estate. His suggestion was that she apply for a cashiering position at the JC Penney department store at our local mall.

The real estate market was booming right then and the recession was still almost two years away, so I couldn't understand why anyone would be having difficulty making a good living in residential real estate. She was friendly and outgoing and knowledgeable, based on more than two decades of experience.

I asked her if she was "farming," an expression used to describe the process of choosing a geographical location and staying in contact with its residents on a regular basis. A "farm" typically consisted of three to five hundred homes in the area of your community you knew well and served.

She answered, "I don't want to knock on doors every Saturday."

I thought for a moment and answered, "You only need to do that four times a year."

She was silent for a moment before answering, "I'm listening."

In that moment I got creative and became a problem solver to help my new friend. Two days later I had put together a few pages on this topic of real estate farming that I shared with her. Two weeks later I had written it up as a fifty page eBook that I sold on my website for several years, updating and expanding it a couple of times and raising the price each time.

And the story has a very happy ending. She still lives in the same city as I do, but in a different house with a new husband who is kinder and gentler. Her children are grown and doing well. And she's a top producer in her real estate office and still loves the business of real estate.

What do you know that others don't and that you may well be taking for granted? How can you be creative in your approach to sharing your knowledge and experience as you solve a problem for people that want and need your help?

The youngest cousins wake me up early to say goodbye before they leave for summer school. We have pancakes and grits and fresh squeezed orange juice and I marvel at their enthusiasm and interest in what I am working on in my business. I gift them each two of my books, allowing them to choose the titles. Perhaps one of them will follow in my footsteps, but that will be entirely up to them and not because I initiate the idea. I know better than that.

# Section Four - Clear Roads Ahead

*If the sight of blue skies fills you with joy, if the simple things of nature have a message you understand, rejoice, for your soul is alive.*
~ Eleonora Duse

I pull into Cook Out, a hamburger joint in Kingsport where I will meet a long time client for the first time in person. I'm early and this place is on Stone Drive, surrounded by a dozen other fast food places that are typical of the south. My first thought is that in California you would never have so many choices for greasy food so close together. But I'm in Tennessee and this is par for the course and not for me to judge.

My client has told me she will be coming with her adult daughter. I'm sitting down on one of the benches just inside the front door when they come in. It turns out she and I are both using canes today and we motion to each other by lifting them an eighth of an inch off the floor in unison. We all hug and make our way to a table.

This is a joyous situation for me, where I can spend time face to face with someone who has been on my list for years, has purchased many of my books, products, and online courses and has greatly benefitted from them in terms of using my concepts and strategies to build her own profitable business online. Her daughter had been skeptical at first, but now sees that I am a real person who cares about the people I serve. I watch as her attitude shifts and she begins to ask me questions about how she can become a part of the business with her mother.

These are two very intelligent women who have experienced life in a very different way than I have. It is always important for me to stay connected with people so that I can better understand their perspective and goals for starting and building an online business and better serve them over time.

We discuss my client's business in great detail and I share ideas and insights as to how she can grow it more quickly now that she has a solid foundation. What I love is that her niche emerged as an extension of who she is and what she loves. Now she has also authored several books on her topic and has begun selling related physical products online as well.

It turns out her grandson is an employee at Cook Out, but she makes it clear there will be no free French fries. After a couple of hours of way too much greasy food we drive off in opposite directions. I am smiling and so glad to have had time with these people. They are the reason I love what I am doing in my business.

# I Can See for Miles and Miles

*I'm looking through you, where did you go?*
*I thought I knew you, what did I know?*
*You don't look different, but you have changed;*
*I'm looking through you, you're not the same.*
*~ The Beatles, "I'm Looking Through You"*

I'm now headed northeast on Interstate 81 through and past the tri-cities of Kingsport and Johnson City, Tennessee and Bristol, Virginia. My destination later today is the home of clients in Charlottesville, Virginia but they aren't expecting me until suppertime. I'm happy to take it easy driving through Virginia and stopping in Roanoke and several other smaller towns along the way. This area is rich in history I know little about, except through textbooks and documentary films and I am ready to be educated by immersing myself in it fully.

Just as I entertain yet another thought about the rain, or the lack of it during this trip so far large droplets slowly begin to appear on my windshield. At first I think they are dust smudges from driving my car for over a week without a wash, but quickly I see that I am driving in the rain.

As the gentle rain turns into a full on downpour I remember that my birthday is tomorrow. This makes me sad for a moment and I'm not sure why. Maybe I will share this with my client in Charlottesville, but I certainly do not want to put her and her family on the spot. I finally decide this year will be a private birthday celebration that I will remember forever and write about in a book almost three years later, although I don't know that at the time. This book is that book.

I often describe a day during April of 2005 as the day I could finally see my life clearly. That morning I woke up to a warm spring day and all of my senses were magnified. It was as if something had overtaken me while I was sleeping and now the colors were more vivid, the sounds more acute, and the food laden with just the right spices to seduce my taste buds. These sensations did not frighten me in the least, but instead served as a confirmation that I was going to be able to change my life completely, first by changing my thoughts and beliefs and second by taking massive action in a direction that would serve my needs and propel me forward in a way I had not experienced in my lifetime.

At that moment my vision for my future was clear, but not fleshed out into a workable plan with legs. I was aware of this and kept my thinking moving forward in a direction that would attract the right people and circumstances into my life. I had the confidence and a strong faith in what I was doing and believed that everything would work itself out over time. Also, in that moment I became infinitely patient and trusted God and the universe to lead me forward towards joy and success.

You vision for your life and business will come to you over time if you allow it all to unfold effortlessly. Yes, you must take action and do the work but you must also allow the magic and creativity to flow through you and into your life experience.

I have already mentioned some business models you will want to consider, including affiliate marketing, product creation, and marketing for small businesses in your community. Let's take a closer look at each of these so you can have a better idea of which of these makes sense for you and for your goals.

Affiliate marketing is the process of recommending products, courses, and services you have purchased, used, and benefitted from in exchange for a commission. The commission rates vary, but digital products, courses, and services tend to be at least thirty to fifty percent of the purchase price. Physical products earn you much less in commissions, but are also excellent to recommend to others who will also benefit from purchasing them for their own use.

For example, you can be an affiliate for my products and courses and I will pay you a commission for each sale. You may also be an affiliate for a site like Amazon and earn commissions for books and almost anything else you can imagine. The possibilities are almost endless and you will have immediate access to an unlimited inventory of products that you do not need to create, fulfill, or follow up with in terms of customer service. There is no doubt this model is the most effective and extremely popular for those new to entrepreneurship.

When I began as an online entrepreneur in 2006 the idea of affiliate marketing was foreign to most companies and businesses. This all changed within the next several years and now you may earn affiliate commission by recommending athletic wear, DNA testing kits, gyms, and almost anything you can imagine. I love that this business model has gone more mainstream during this past decade.

The product creation model is one in which you create a product based on the knowledge and information you have on a specific topic. For some reason I found this confusing at the beginning of my entrepreneurial journey, whereas now I have embraced the idea wholeheartedly.

My first information product was an eBook (this was before Kindle and other Amazon publishing) on the topic of real estate farming. I mentioned this story earlier in Chapter 9 (Meet the Cousins). It was inspired by a neighbor whose husband wanted her to get a "real" job unless she could earn more income as a real estate agent. I had worked in real estate for twenty years before coming online and I asked her if she was farming. This is the process of adopting a neighborhood and then serving them over time in various ways. When she said she was not and I saw that she did not even understand the concept I created my product on what had worked for me during all of those years. She continued working in real estate and I sold lots of eBooks.

An information product can also be delivered as a live training, within a membership site, or as an online course.

Local business marketing involves working closely with a brick and mortar business to help them make the phone ring. I began by helping a family member get the word out about his new handyman business without having to spend hundreds of dollars each month on newspaper and magazine advertising.

When I was successful with this and enjoyed the work and the results I was getting I then reached out to other small business owners in my community to help them in a similar way. While I no longer take on small businesses to market for in this way, over the past decade I have enjoyed helping insurance agents, dentists, a handyman, chiropractors, plumbers, and others in various professions and trades to make their phone rings so their businesses would thrive.

At some point I began marketing for the non-profits I am a part of in both of the cities where I live, first on a pro bono basis and later as a paid consultant. It is extremely rewarding to help with fundraising for causes you deeply believe in and to then watch them flourish.

# Meet the Clients

*Make it a habit to tell people thank you, without the expectation of anything in return.*
*Appreciate those around you, and you'll soon find many others around you.*
~ Ralph Marston

The last time I drove through the state of Virginia from the west end to the east end and top to bottom was more than thirty years ago. I was married with two young stepkids at that time, truly a lifetime ago.

Back then I was also a serious photographer. While I was a student at UCLA I photographed other students who wanted to be working actors. The joke in those days was that everyone at UCLA wanted to be in show business; half wanted to act and the other half had dreams of writing, producing, or directing.

My dream was to write but I did not take the necessary action to even give myself a chance. I failed in the sense that I did not take it far enough to be rejected. This was because I did not complete enough work to even be in the game. No effort equaled no results. This was a hard lesson that I did not turn around until coming online in 2006. I will spend the remainder of my life in an attempt to make up for lost time; even though I am satisfied completely with the way my life has unfolded.

As I drive through the Virginia countryside almost everything I gaze upon looks and feels familiar. Even though I am tired from waking up so many times last night because of the pain from the sciatica I still find myself pulling over or taking an exit to see more of what this beautiful area has to offer. Every photograph I take on my iPhone reminds me of the ones I took in these locations with my Nikon F2 with a noisy motor drive so very long ago. How times have changed over the passing decades, and not just with technology.

My client has recently moved from the thriving, artistic, and culturally alive city of Charlottesville out to the countryside of Crozet, Virginia. Crozet is not a city or town, but instead is referred to as a "census-designated place" - a concentration of population defined by the United States Census Bureau for statistical purposes only and possessing no legal status. I was not familiar with this concept until I knew I would be visiting and did some research online beforehand.

Census-designated-places or CDPs as they are now referred as have been used in each decennial census since 1980 as the counterparts of incorporated places, such as self-governing cities, towns, and villages, for the purposes of gathering and correlating statistical data. They are populated areas that generally include one officially designated but currently unincorporated small community, for which the CDP is named, plus surrounding inhabited countryside of varying dimensions and, occasionally, other, smaller unincorporated communities as well. CDPs include small rural communities, colonias located along the U.S. border with Mexico, and unincorporated resort and retirement communities and their environs. There are just over five thousand inhabitants in this CDP community of Crozet.

As I make my way east on Interstate 64 where it intersects with I-81 the terrain becomes even more lush. I pull off at a scenic stop to take some photos and to inhale the awesomeness of the breathtaking view. I also call my client to let her know where I am and that I will be at her house in about an hour. She is excited to hear my voice and tells me that her family can't wait to meet me as they begin returning home that evening. I also share that I have injured myself and that I will need to stay on the first floor. By the hesitation in her voice I can assume the room they had ready for my two day stay is on the second floor. I promise to not be a bother and tell her even the sofa is perfect for me. Back on the road now to stay on my schedule.

Two hours later I finally admit I am lost. I am somewhere between Crozet Crossing and Three Notched Road and my car's navigation system is thoroughly confused. The sun is going down and I call for help. My client comes to meet me and I follow her into the forest and to the end of the road, where there are only three homes. It's like an enchanted forest and I am transported into mythical times found only in storybooks and fairy tales. I understand completely why she and her family were willing to move so far away from civilization to live this unique experience.

I put my things down in the living room, which will serve as the guest room for my stay. Then she and I go into her office and get to work before her husband comes home from work, her daughters return after their after school activities have concluded, and her mother-in-law is dropped off from the adult day care facility she attends two or three times each week. Three generations have come together for this family's life experience and my goal is to help my client to maneuver and navigate in a way that will serve her goals while also allowing her to be there for her husband, mother-in-law, and three teenage daughters.

The husband is employed by a large corporation about a forty-five minute drive east of here into Charlottesville. He can't imagine any other life and prefers to focus on the benefits of his work rather than thinking about any limitations. His mother is now having some memory issues and has recently moved in with them for added assistance, companionship, and enrichment. The girls are in middle and high school and very busy with academics, sports, and music.

This leaves my client in the precarious position of having five people to look after in some way before she can focus on herself and her clients each day. The result is that she is behind on every project she has committed to and stays up until well after midnight at least twice a week in order to catch up. It's exhausting and unproductive as well as financially devastating if this continues. My goal is to have several family meetings while I am here to help facilitate this transition from mother, wife, caregiver to home-based entrepreneur as smoothly as possible.

Her office is just off the living room and allows for both an excellent view of the lush forest as well as for privacy. I can only imagine how gorgeous it is during the snowy winter months. She shows me around and then we settle in to do some planning. I am an expert in time management and productivity and have facilitated effective change and growth with clients who heed my specific advice for their situations. My client has the potential to earn about a half million dollars a year in her business, yet she struggles to earn even six figures each year.

We make a list of the clients she is currently working with, as well as the tasks and activities she performs for each of them. We add all of this information to a white board in her office that can be seen from anywhere else in the room. Then we write down her schedule to discover when she has time completely to herself and how that can be expanded.

It turns out that there are three weekdays where she is home alone for a total of twenty-four hours a week. We then add in four hours on Saturday when everyone else is busy with activities that do not require her presence. This leaves every day after four o'clock, mornings until eight, and the remainder of Saturday and all day Sunday for her to spend time with one or more of her family members. She laughs and says that she sees it in print but it still feels as if she will not be able to make this plan and schedule come to fruition.

At that moment her fourteen year old daughter comes in to the office and is already in the middle of a sentence when I interrupt.

"Is she allowed to do this?" I ask, pointing to the girl, now silent and frozen in place. I continue to maintain eye contact with my client.

"Not any longer," she answers, not breaking her steady gaze into my eyes.

I invite her daughter to sit down with us and she explains that if she doesn't tell her mother what she is thinking right away she will forget. She and my client follow me into the kitchen where I find a magnetic white board on the side of the refrigerator. If she writes down what she wanted to say, then when mom comes out of her office she can take a look and address the issue. They both nod in agreement that this is an excellent solution. I am a problem solver and love empowering others to solve perceived problems as well.

We all have some meaningful conversations during my stay and everyone is on board with the small tweaks we have come up with to ensure my client has the time she needs to accomplish her work each day. But the most important part of our time together occurred while we discussed how she could enhance her sales skills and powers of persuasion.

Mastering the skills of salesmanship and persuasion will turn you into an unstoppable entrepreneur. Easier said than done, this is most definitely worth your time and effort to study, practice, and master. These skills are the most valuable ones you can possess as an entrepreneur, in my opinion. If you are able to sell yourself, your products, and your services you will always be able to earn an excellent living. Add persuasion techniques to your repertoire and you will become super human in both your life and your business.

Become an astute observer of your own and other people's buying behavior. How and why does someone make a decision to buy or not buy something, whether it's digital or physical and regardless of the price? When you can answer that question in regards to your own products and services you will close more sales and earn more money as a direct result.

My client is a gifted writer, editor, and teacher. What she lacks is the ability to sell herself and to persuade others to take advantage of what she has to offer.

We spend hours in her office going through her Rolodex of clients. It reads like a "Who's Who" of the elite, prominent authors and entrepreneurs of our time. We discuss how she came to know each of them and what these relationships look like.

Then I think back to when she first contacted me. We had met while I was speaking at Joe Vitale's live event in Austin, Texas several years earlier. She was attending the event and had a table in the back of the room where she could speak with people who were interested in writing and editing books.

She sent me an email about a year later. If she hadn't included her photo I would not have recognized her just from seeing her name. In the message she said that she believed she had something to offer the people who were attending my upcoming event and that she would like to have the opportunity to be one of my speakers. We had a short phone call and I invited her to attend and present to my group.

At that time she had courage and confidence, and it is my goal to help her and everyone I work with to regain that feeling that comes from knowing who you are and what your purpose and goals are for your life and business. It all comes together when you are able to sell others on yourself and what you have to offer, to the point they are anxious to work with you and believe it was their idea from the very beginning.

## Three Qualities of an Effective Sales Person

Confidence is the first quality and accounts for the highest percentage of success stories for entrepreneurs, in my experience. When I left my job as a classroom teacher my confidence and self-esteem were at an all time low. I allowed the unkind remarks from some of the administrators and other teachers get to me and whittle away at my psyche. The result was that I honestly believed that I was not capable of achieving my goals and dreams. I did not realize just how deeply I had been affected until I had the opportunity to evaluate my thinking and belief system during my first year away from that job and working for myself as an entrepreneur.

These days my confidence is higher than it has ever been before and I make a concerted effort to boost the confidence of everyone I come in contact with each day.

Empathy is the second piece of this process. Possessing the capacity to understand or feel what another person is experiencing from within their frame of reference, that is, the capacity to place oneself in another's position will help you to make more sales. If someone is still working at a job that no longer serves them and hopes for a different life, I can go to that place in my own mind and pull up my experiences in thoughts and feelings and then understand almost exactly what they are going through.

The ability to make a point by telling a story is the third prong of this strategy to become the best sales person you can be. When I was in junior high school we lived next door to a family with four children. There were three boys, with only about a year between each of them and then a little girl, about five years younger than the youngest of the boys. The middle brother, Tory was my best friend at that time and his mother and little sister would often walk over to our house to call him home for dinner.

Little Katherine would regularly say to my mother "Why do you have so many stories?" to which she would answer "You'll have lots of stories too when you grow up."

I didn't give this much thought at the time, but the truth is that we all learn and grow through the telling of stories.

Have confidence in what you do. Exercise empathy and compassion for the people you encounter. Share poignant and relevant stories about what is possible. Then close the sale and begin to serve your new client in the best way possible.

# From Sea to Shining Sea

*Together we can face any challenges, deep as the ocean and as high as the sky.*
~ Sonia Gandhi

From Crozet I head east to Woodbridge, Virginia, bouncing back and forth between state highways to see as much as possible. I'm only about a hundred twenty miles to where my next clients are waiting for me and I take my time driving through the lush green countryside. Standardsville to Ruckersville to Gordonsville to Chancellorsville. Then over to Fredericksburg and up Interstate 95 to my destination in Woodbridge.

As I continue on this journey I think back to years long past, when I drove the I-95 corridor more regularly. Living in Miami as a teenager and young adult took me on that road up to Georgia many times to see family, and other times all the way up to Philadelphia and New York as my horizons broadened and I was seeking greener pastures to conquer.

I pull over to send a text to my clients and they are waiting in front of their house as I pull into the driveway five minutes later. I've told them that I hurt my leg and they raise their eyebrows as they watch me get out of the car to greet them. There are five steps leading up to the front door and I take them slowly and carefully.

Over the next two days we engage in a variety of activities, including a trip to the neighborhood grocery store where I am able to drive a motorized cart in order to do my shopping. Those carts make a huge difference for people with mobility issues and this is the first time I fully appreciate them from a personal perspective. We also attend the local Rotary meeting where my clients have been members for longer than I have been a Rotarian.

These are people I have worked with for several years now in my mentoring program and with whom I have also shared the stage in Toronto and London. They are also bestselling authors of a book on real estate investing, an area they specialize in and train others to be successful with by following their proven strategies. They have come to me to learn more about online entrepreneurship.

We have chosen the niche of public speaking for them to get started with online, as they both have extensive experience in this area. This includes teaching others how to get started as speakers, improve their speaking, and bring their speaking online with webinars and podcasts. There are in the midst of creating an online course as an introductory product. While I am here we will write the sales copy, have the technical setup completed, and get their new information product ready for sale. Yes, an online course can be created fairly quickly when you are focused and determined.

They watch intently as I labor with each step in order to join them at the dining room table, and I know they are silently thanking God they are of sound body at this time. They work harder than I expected and I am sure this is because they see how much pain I am in. Sometimes we all need a reminder of the areas of our life we may be taking for granted, like being able to move about physically without having to give that a second thought.

I'm used to hearing complaints from many of my clients as to how difficult it is to choose a niche, come up with an idea for a product or course, get the technical pieces of setting up a site and connecting the payment processor, and then marketing it to the right people, but with these clients today there is only gratitude at our table.

In the big scheme of things entrepreneurship is not difficult. Everything is relative to where you are right now and we must be grateful and thankful for what we have at all times. There is delicious take-out food on the kitchen counter and they prepare a plate for me. We push on, break for the evening, and complete the product by the next morning.

There are people around the world who will benefit from learning from you, and whom can only learn from you because of the way you share the knowledge and experience you possess. When you teach another person what you know you have touched their heart and soul in a way that cannot ever be taken away. Think about your business in this way and you will be forever blessed as an entrepreneur. It's all about serving others.

There will be bumps along the way and that is when you "course correct" as quickly as you can. Every mistake or misstep is the opportunity for you to learn even more and to proceed with confidence and courage. If you manage to avoid these bumps in the road or to ignore them when they do show up, you are cheating yourself out of the most powerful experiences life has to offer and a priceless education in the process. Embrace the imperfections and be creative and innovative in how you move past them.

On my last morning we drive past the Occoquan Bay National Wildlife Refuge and continue down to Leesylvania State Park. It sits on the shores of the Potomac River and I can see all the way across to where I will be headed next - Maryland and Washington, D.C. It's only fifty miles to where my next client lives in Bowie, Maryland but the drive will take almost three hours because of the traffic.

As I make my way slowly through Virginia and in to Maryland I think about the fact that I have now come three thousand miles and will soon be where I can see the Atlantic Ocean. I have driven from sea to shining sea during these past couple of weeks, and oh how my outlook and perspective on life has changed after dealing with my sciatica and spending time with some of my clients. I wouldn't trade anything in the world for this experience.

# Section Five - Stuck in the Middle

*If you find yourself stuck in the middle there is only one way to go; forward.*
~ Richard Branson

This morning I have the Stealers Wheel song "Stuck in the Middle" stuck in my head. You may recognize it:

*Clowns to the left of me,*
*Jokers to the right, here I am,*
*Stuck in the middle with you.*

I'm not in the middle of the United States, far from it, but I am at the halfway point in my road trip. So in that sense I am stuck in the middle of a journey that I both looked forward to and now realize was quite an undertaking for one person, even without having the pain from sciatica since day three. But I look myself square in the eye in the rearview mirror and say out loud,

"I'm Connie Ragen Green and I can do anything. I have overcome more challenges and obstacles throughout my life than almost anyone I know and I have emerged victorious."

I smile and see how tired I look today. I've aged a little during this trip, but with that has come some wisdom and enlightenment, I believe.

Perseverance is what has made the difference for me, I believe. Early on I became aware of the fact that many people would start an online business with high hopes and sincere intentions, only to abandon their websites and projects a short time later. If I could simply stay the course I would be successful! This was a great gift in that I let go of many of my feelings and beliefs around my inadequacies and limitations and got to work. That strategy paid off quickly and continue to do so.

With that I put the car into gear and head towards the town of Bowie. Decades ago I knew a couple in California and the wife had grown up in Bowie. Her father was a podiatrist and her mother worked on the Bowie Blade, the local newspaper. I knew they had a race track there that has since closed and is now used as a training center for thoroughbred horses. Until I began working with my client who lives here a few years ago I do not believe I have ever heard the name of the city mentioned in the years in between.

The traffic in and around Washington, D.C. is more than I had bargained for. It's Friday morning and I get caught between three Interstates in order to make my way to the highway I need that will lead me into Maryland. Then, in a split second I have a flashback. It all comes back to me now.

All those years ago, as I was driving through this exact area with my first husband we were stuck in this same traffic pattern. The beltways are confusing and misleading to out-of-towners in that they simply go 'round and 'round and you cannot easily get over six lanes to pick up your exit. Even though my navigation system is talking to me (I have it set up with an Australian woman's voice; I have named her "Victoria") to guide me in the right direction I miss it twice and finally feel the pain increasing in my lower back and down my left leg due to this added stress. I'm stuck in the middle of our nation's capitol and I simply can't take it anymore.

I exit where I'm at and drive into a residential area. The roar of the highway is still ringing in my ears. I see a public library and dart into its parking lot. Once I have found a spot I call my client and tell her I am lost and to please come to me instead of us meeting at the restaurant she has picked out.

I decide to go into the library to use the restroom while I am waiting, but they have no ramp on this side of the building and I am too tired to walk or even drive around to the front. So I limp up the stairs, taking each one slowly and carefully and feeling a little bit sorry for my situation. My client said she would meet me down the street at a park in thirty minutes so I am able to take my time before going to meet her.

Twenty minutes later and I am still maneuvering the stairway from where the bathroom is located in the basement of the library to the first level where my car is parked in the lot. The elevator is at the front of the building, much too far for me to walk around. How do people who are disabled get around at this library? I am thinking and maybe I even say this out loud. I have taken my mobility for granted for most of my life and wonder what else I am clueless about in our world when it comes to humanity.

By the time I get back out to my car I see that I am running late by a few minutes and by the time I start the engine my cell phone rings. It is my client, frantic about my whereabouts. Yes, I am fine. No, I did not drive down to the park yet. Yes, I think I heard an ambulance go by a few minutes ago, but I was in the basement of the library so maybe I didn't hear it. I'm not sure.

It turns out someone collapsed at the park and as she was driving up to meet me the ambulance was taking them away. The person matched my description and she was sure it had been me. She drives to the library and we are still on the phone when she pulls into the lot and past my car.

This client is one I have known and worked with for years. She is also one of the most intelligent people I know. But I have grown to think of her as a sister for yet another quality she possesses; she is an incredibly kind and caring human being and that trumps most other descriptions of a person's character and makeup, in my opinion. I am so looking forward to our time together over the next two days.

I follow her to a restaurant just a few minutes away. She has invited another friend who will join us for lunch.

## Outsourcing and Scalability

Years ago when I was a new online entrepreneur I insisted on answering emails and handling my own customer service. My mentor at that time insisted this was not scalable as my business grew and that it must be outsourced to someone who would serve my customers, prospects, and clients in the way I would want them to be treated.

I begged to differ and insisted on continuing to do this myself. I still do this to a large extent to this day, but I also understand why my mentor was so adamant about his beliefs on this topic. At this point I have more than a dozen people assisting me in my business in some capacity. And sometimes we do not fully understand what someone is attempting to teach us until we are in the position of teaching that same concept to someone else.

My client is accomplished in the corporate world, and as she approached her fiftieth birthday she began to have a vision for a different life for herself and her family. As I shared earlier, there is many times a catalyst to someone wanting to leave the traditional workforce and starting their own business as an entrepreneur.

After almost three decades of travel on short notice, layoffs, coworkers who did not do their fair share of the projects she was in charge of completing, and so much more the idea of being able to work from home or from wherever she happened to be in the world and replace her current income was quite appealing.

She began sharing her knowledge of technology with the world of new entrepreneurs, published a bestselling book, taught online courses on a variety of topics, and became a public speaker. Then she dabbled in physical products that could be sold on Amazon, eBay, and other sites and discovered this was her true passion.

I was mentoring her from the beginning of this part of her journey and watched as she grew this business to profitable margins with brilliant strategies. Then I watched as she began to shrink under a mountain of physical products in her living room, with no one there to assist her. We had many discussions about scaling her business and outsourcing some of the tasks involved, but she was not open to exploring these avenues. She was stuck in between launching and growing this business and scaling it to be able to sustain steady growth. It was painful to see a business implode due to a few missteps but it was an inevitable next step in her journey.

It's true, no one will take care of your business and clients like you will. But the secret is that there are many people who will handle it all much better than you ever could! Once I began allowing others to do some of the work required in my business for me, I was able to grow exponentially.

Soon I figured out that anything that was technical or clerical in nature was better off done by someone else. This freed me up to only do each day the tasks and activities I loved and was good at. These continue to include writing, creating products and courses, marketing, teaching and public speaking, and mentoring. I also do some corporate consulting, which is a combination of marketing and teaching people at the three corporations who currently hire me to consult with them.

My specific area of expertise is with online marketing and many times I will fly in for a day or two to show them in person how to reach their prospects and customers in ways that are innovative and unique to their industry.

My recommendations to this client were that she limit her activities to the research and sourcing of products to sell online, and to writing the sales copy for each one. She would outsource the packaging and shipping of all items and oversee the bookkeeping involved to keep track of sales. Leasing a small office a few miles from her home to house the products as they were delivered and shipped, and hiring two people part-time to handle the packing and shipping of these products to the various distribution centers makes sense. I calculated the cost of all of this to be approximately three thousand dollars a month and believed that this would be an excellent investment in what could have become a seven figure a year business.

This did not happen and within a year and a half of my visit she was forced to close her business, except for some smaller items she continued to do from home. It is heartbreaking to watch this happen, but entrepreneurs can be stubborn and single-minded when it comes to giving up control of every aspect of their business. She was literally "stuck in the middle" between working in her business every moment and enjoying successful entrepreneurship by handing off some of the pieces that would be better done by employees and independent contractors.

My advice is for you to find a mentor you trust and follow their recommendations step by step to see how it feels for you. The saying is "if you don't have an assistant, you are one" and this definitely applies in this case. You may be telling yourself that you are the only person who can do some of the tasks and activities involved, but that is seldom true if you take a closer look and allow others to do the same. The magic comes when you discover that others can do some of what you do so much faster, easier, and more cost effectively than you are doing right now.

# The Psychology of Entrepreneurship

*I'm convinced that about half of what separates successful entrepreneurs from the non-successful ones is pure perseverance.*
~ Steve Jobs

As I am driving away from Bowie, Maryland and headed towards Fredericksburg, Virginia on my way south I think about what I refer to as the psychology of entrepreneurship. There is a very real, psychological component to entrepreneurship that is seldom discussed. I will share more on this topic later on, but suffice it to say that many times we engage in passive aggressive behavior and self-sabotage our own success. You are not likely to recognize this until someone else points it out to you, and by then it may be too late for your business to recover. Make it a point to learn from other people's mistakes instead of choosing to learn the hard way on your own.

Using my own experiences as an example, I will share that I started as an online entrepreneur in late 2005 and into 2006 with the belief that I was not *enough* to be successful. This expanded into not smart enough, not young enough, not likeable enough, not business-minded enough, not attractive enough, not connected enough, and many more *not enoughs.* While this was not the reality of my situation, because I had gone from thinking and believing certain things to having results based on what I thought and believed at the time, this was my reality. Allow me to explain further.

Looking back at what my life was like during the 1990s it's difficult to believe I accomplished as much as I did. My mind was programmed for failure on many levels. Several months before I resigned from my teaching position and gave away my best real estate clients I began attending workshops and conferences that were intended as self-improvement and personal growth trainings.

It was there where I learned about the mind and how we choose the life we create for ourselves. The cycle goes like this...

**Thoughts => Feelings => Beliefs => Actions => Results**

When I thought I was not smart enough to start an online business it made me feel small and insecure. This led to a belief that I could not achieve my goal. My actions were those of someone who doesn't think they can do anything well, and my results proved it all to be true with concrete validation. From someone more advanced in their thinking, looking in at my life from their perspective it made sense that my life was a struggle both personally and professionally.

As I began to understand more about this I became open to learning and putting into practice the principles that were being shared with me. It would all begin with changing the thoughts I was thinking. Easier said than done, I soon found out. I continued to think that changing my life was not possible. When I explored this thought more closely, the full thought was that I honestly believed I could not change my life unless I had an almost endless supply of money. If money were not an object anything would be possible in my life.

Having a large balance in my bank account would make me feel like I could make choices not based around my job as a teacher and my real estate business. In turn, I would then believe that I could take the time to explore alternative methods of earning a living, doing the things I thought I loved.

How did I achieve this? I pretended to have a million dollars in my bank account! Now I didn't write any checks or pledge large donations to a charity, but in the subconscious recesses of my mind I was a millionaire.

Then I went further. My teaching job was not going well and I didn't want to be there every day. So one morning as I was getting out of my car and walking in from the parking lot to my classroom I had a thought that first made me get goose bumps all over and then made me feel warm and comforted.

The teachers always said that if they were being paid more they would be more than willing to do more. I did not believe this and thought that at any job you do as much as you can because it is the proper thing to do.

What if I were being paid one million dollars a year, after taxes, to do my teaching job? How would that change what I did and how I did it.

As I entered my classroom and closed the door I stood in the dark for several minutes before turning on the lights. It felt wonderful to know I was being paid so well for doing a job I continued to love when it came to working with my students. I thought about the work I did before and after school, as well as on the weekends. I suddenly realized I resented having to do that because I had so much else to do in my personal life and in my real estate business. I always completed this additional work but in a begrudging way.

Then I smiled. If I were receiving one million dollars a year, wouldn't I be thrilled to spend much of my free time doing more? And I could afford to pay specialists to come in to my classroom to assist me. Nothing would be too much for the administration to ask of me under these circumstances.

Once I had tricked my mind into believing this thought I could feel the shift in my whole life. My body was lighter and I no longer carried the weight of the world on my shoulders. That week I brought my neighbor's trash and recycling bins from the street into the area next to her house because she was having some health issues and it was a nice thing to do. I baked some cookies and left them anonymously in the teacher's lunchroom. And I arranged to have someone I knew who had written for two television shows come in once a week to help me teach writing in my classroom, and paid him to do so.

The change in me was obvious to the other teachers and the principal almost immediately. My mood was lighter and I wasn't taking myself or anything that occurred so seriously. I began offering my help to others and after being suspicious at first they finally took me up on my offers.

Within a few weeks the principal was telling people what an excellent job I was doing in the classroom and one day she said this to me while we were surrounded by other teachers, some parents, and my students.

That would be my last year in the classroom and I did my best. Not the "best" I thought was the right thing to do, but the best that could be done based on my skills, abilities, resources, and willingness to better my best with this and every other situation in my life. I would never again engage in passive aggressive behavior and sabotage my success. This was no longer a part of my make-up and was not in my thoughts, feelings, beliefs, or actions. I knew this to be true by looking at my results.

# Perfectly Imperfect

*Love your curves and all your edges;*
*All your perfect imperfections*
From "All of Me", written and performed by John Legend

Perfectionism can rear its ugly head at almost any time in our lives. The child who suddenly melts down when they receive less than a perfect score on a math or spelling test; the athlete that quits the team after missing the mark on a play they have been working on for years; the writer who stops writing when a critic points out a flaw in their story. All of these are examples of how crippling perfectionism can be when we allow it to get out of hand.

I was positive that I was not a perfectionist until I was called out by a social worker in 1994. I was preparing to become a foster parent and we were doing a final walkthrough of my home before I would be eligible to receive a child in protective custody for an extended period of time.

We were in the living room discussing something I no longer remember and she said to me,

"Remember, these children are coming from chaotic, dysfunctional situations. You're a perfectionist and no child will be able to meet your standards."

I'm sure my mouth fell open for a moment before I answered.

"I'm not a perfectionist. Look around; nothing here is perfect."

Without uttering another word she spoke volumes to me that day. I could have been stubborn and dismissed her observation as being based on information she did not fully understand. But instead, I chose to believe that she had experience in this area and had noticed some things I was unaware of at that time. I thanked her for coming and immediately after she drove away I sat down to think about what she had said.

I have to say she did me a huge favor by pointing out what she had observed in knowing me during the previous several months. Could it be that the course of my life had been altered due to my perfectionist tendencies? Taking out my notebook, I wrote down what I thought she meant. Yes, I expected things to be done completely and properly? Was that so wrong? Yes, I was critical at times when things were not done correctly the first time. But had I ever expressed this, directly or indirectly to the children I taught or to people in my life?

It would be years before I fully addressed this issue and abandoned perfectionism in favor of excellence, but the seed had been planted and I had this thought at the back of my mind each day as I interacted with others.

The following morning we meet with another client at a restaurant in Baltimore. This other client lives south of Baltimore in a city I am not familiar with. It's so much fun to spend almost two hours in conversation with these two women. I try to hide the fact that I am in great pain but I'm sure they see right through the facade. By noon we hug and go our separate ways.

A half hour later I'm in horrible traffic and it will take me nine hours to drive the three hundred fifty miles to Fayetteville, North Carolina where I will spend the night. This adventure involves a ferret in the swimming pool and a hotel room out of a Stephen King story.

Ferrets are two to three pound furry mammals of the same genus as weasels. I love all of God's creatures great and small but sometimes there is a caveat. Ferrets are crepuscular, meaning that they spend about fourteen to eighteen hours a day asleep and are most active around the hours of dawn and dusk. Unlike their solitary polecat ancestors, most ferrets will live happily in social groups. A group of ferrets is commonly referred to as a "business". They are territorial, like to burrow, and prefer to sleep in an enclosed area.

So when I pulled into the parking lot at the motel in Fayetteville and see a crowd at the pool I know something is up before I ever see slinky wet creatures weaving in and out of people's legs and an odd splashing in the water.

I parked in front of the office and the lady at the desk was wearing a big smile. When she saw how difficult it was for me to get out of my car she came out from behind the desk quickly. Arms outstretched, she took my purse in one hand and my arm in the other to make it easier for me. Today's long drive had taken its toll on me and I was most appreciative of her help.

"They come from all over on Saturday nights. There's nothing much to do around these parts so the swimming pool is kind of the big attraction."

It was Saturday night, June twenty-fifth and here I was in North Carolina, enjoying the warm, humid weather and ready for a good night's sleep.

"It looks like they are really having fun."

I shifted my body in the direction of the pool and could now see there were people of all ages, some in the pool and others standing at the edge, and there were those little creatures again. They were furry and shiny in the water and slithering all over. I pointed and was about to ask a question when she said,

"They're ferrets. We keep 'em as pets. You didn't want to go swimming, did you?"

I shook my head, no, I had no interest in going into the pool, even if it was just filled with humans. This had to be the most interesting situation I had encountered so far on this trip.

She handed me the room key and I just looked at it for a moment. I hadn't seen a key for years and was now used to the coded cards most hotels and motels were using these days. She had given me a room as far away from the pool party as possible. I got back into my car and drove down a ways to park in front of my door. I will spare you the details of what I experienced in my room because I am sure this will become a short story at some point in my future.

The next thing I knew it was Sunday morning.

# Alone Again, Naturally

*All that we see or seem*
*Is but a dream within a dream.*
~ Edgar Allan Poe, A Dream Within a Dream

It's a three hour drive from Fayetteville, North Carolina to my next destination of Rock Hill, South Carolina, and after the excitement at the motel with so many people I welcome the freedom and solitude of the open road once again. This is different from loneliness in that I have everything I need at this moment within the spaces inside of my vehicle. It is relatively quiet, except for the hum of the engine and the motion of the tires rolling across the highway. I am alone with my thoughts and this makes me happy and content.

Today is Sunday, June 26th and my body is stiff from the grind of driving, sleeping in new places almost every night, and from eating more Cracker Barrel food than I had previously believed was humanly possible, at least for this human.

Somewhere between the emergency room in St. Louis and filling the prescriptions in Tennessee I had discovered the magic of Cracker Barrel in terms of easily gathering enough food for lunch and dinner in one stop. Driving was bearable but getting in and out of my car several times each day was painful and finally intolerable so this strategy made perfect sense.

It's funny to think that I turned up my nose at Cracker Barrel food when I passed it in Arizona two weeks ago; now I am scheduling my road trip around finding one to stop at each day by noon. This is how it works...

I pull into the parking lot and take my time getting out of the car. Then I slowly walk into the lobby where there are many items for sale, including food, gifts, and other objects of interest. I decide what I will be taking with me while I am waiting to be seated. My cane is balanced on my left wrist if I need to look more closely at something and I stay aware of my surroundings to make sure no one accidentally bumps in to me.

Once seated I order as quickly as possible. This is authentic southern food based on traditions established many decades ago and I choose the largest meal they have that includes a main dish and three sides. As soon as the server delivers the food to my table I ask for a box to take what I do not eat with me. Then I eat half of what they have brought and carefully box up the remainder for my dinner that evening.

This food is the definition of "comfort" food and I allow it to wrap me in its arms. My favorites include the country fried steak, yams, and buttermilk biscuits. They have different items depending on the day of the week and I choose to be surprised when I order.

Much thought has gone in to this process as it has become increasingly difficult for me to go into a grocery store, even if they have a cart I can use. Stopping for an additional time during each day is out of the question.

Another thing that I find interesting is that minutes before pulling out of my driveway way back on June 14th I had decided to go back inside the house one last time and fill a paper grocery bag with any non-perishable food I had in my kitchen. This included crackers, foil packages of tuna and salmon, and two kinds of nuts. I thought these items would come in handy and it turns out they make it much easier to have a snack by pulling into a rest area or a parking lot without exiting my vehicle. Now they are providing me with sustenance for my survival.

And something else I learned along the way is that caffeine can help alleviate pain in many cases. It works for me so I stop at a drive through Starbucks each morning and then have an easier time of it for those first few hours when my back and legs are so stiff and tight.

Sure enough, as if on cue a billboard for a Cracker Barrel three exits down appears as I round the bend from Carowinds Amusement Park in Charlotte, North Carolina headed towards Rock Hill, South Carolina. My first husband and I had taken the kids to Carowinds one summer during the late 1970s and I smile as I am reminded of these memories. We were city slickers compared to the people we encountered that week, with nearly everyone speaking in an exaggerated southern drawl. This includes prolongation of the most heavily stressed syllables, with the corresponding weakening of the less stressed ones, so that there is an appearance of slowness from the speaker. One teenager we met during that visit claimed to be from upstate New York, but his drawl said otherwise. We had all found that to be extremely funny at the time.

My mouth is watering as I am seated in the dining room and I order the country fried steak with breaded fried okra, green beans, and the Sunday special side of boiled cabbage. I gobble down less than half of what they bring as I fill up my to-go box with what I will enjoy for dinner.

I try to focus on the positive aspects of this trip as I strain to get back into the car and head to my motel room just outside of the town of Rock Hill, South Carolina. Alone once again in the car and then in my motel my room is a comfortable state of mind and body for me.

# Positioning Yourself

*We are all experts in our own little niches.*
~ Alex Trebek

It's bright and early when I check out of my motel room on Monday morning. I pack up everything I have taken into the room with me last evening and put it back in its place in the back of my Honda Pilot. I drive to where I will meet with three entrepreneurs for the next two days to help them first define and then move forward with their goals.

I have long time friends with whom I am now working with, as well as a new client in Rock Hill and have decided to spend time with everyone simultaneously. My friends are retired teachers who decided to move to Rock Hill from Memphis, Tennessee when their son went through an unpleasant and emotional divorce, in hopes of spending more time with their four grandchildren. They started a graphic design business and I have been their marketing consultant for almost five years now.

My new client is a woman in her forties who started a virtual assistant business last year when she was laid off for the third time in five years. She was ready for a change in her life and came to me to help her reinvent herself as I have done for myself over this past decade.

We have agreed to meet at the Starbucks on Cherry Road to have something to drink and to get acquainted before heading a couple of miles down the road to the Rock Hill Public Auto Auction. My friend has his eye on a BMW and wants to make sure it's still available and didn't sell at yesterday's auction. It's still there and he breathes a sigh of relief as we go back to our cars in the parking lot.

We all head to their home, located in a picturesque area not far from Winthrop University. Once inside I take off my shoes, fire up my iPad, and settle in for an evening of mentoring and marketing with my three students.

Our overall topic is positioning yourself as an expert, something all three of my clients must do in order to build the businesses they have in mind. Once I am able to teach them this process they will take off in their lives and businesses.

## What it Means to "Position Yourself as an Expert"

If you are not familiar with this term, to position yourself as an expert is to take strategic actions that will move you from where you are right now to closer to being thought of as one of the experts and authorities on your niche topic. This is achieved with blogging, authorship, public speaking, and teaching online courses, for the most part. Another piece of this is having others recommend and promote you. The final piece is to take a stand in a controversial area of your niche and work to prove your thinking is correct over a period of years by showing and then telling others what you are doing currently and have already done in the past.

I did this in the areas of list building and relationship marketing by taking a stand and vehemently stating that you do not need a list of ten thousand prospects and clients in order to get to six figures a year in earnings. I was able to achieve this initial income goal with only six hundred fifty-one names on my list in 2008. I began writing about and speaking on this topic, teaching courses based on this premise and concept, and then writing and publishing my first book around this precept in 2010. *Huge Profits with a Tiny List: 50 Ways to Use Relationship Marketing to Increase Your Bottom Line* was well received and put me on the virtual map once it was published.

You cannot rest on your laurels, so once you have achieved expert and authority status in one area it's time to already start climbing the next mountain. Over time this becomes fun and your business will take off like a rocket ship once you get into the rhythm of declaring your precept, showing why it is true, and sharing your results with your community over and over again.

In the case of my clients who now run a graphic design business exclusively online, they began with the premise that everyone can have access to professionally created and uniquely designed graphics at a fair price. They are now in the process of showing their community exactly how this can be done and of assembling a team of graphic designers from around the world who will work with people I refer to as the "graphically challenged" to help us (yes, I am one of these people) to achieve our goals with gorgeous graphics of various types.

This evening we are working together to outline their first book about this work they are doing and tomorrow we will strategize a plan for them to begin speaking locally and to create a simple online course to sell online.

My new client listens intently and silently wonders what I have in mind when it is her turn. I can be quite loud and excitable when I am working with a new entrepreneur on their marketing and this can quickly overwhelm someone who has just met me in person for the first time. My goal is to tone it down, while still maintaining my enthusiasm.

She and I go outside on the porch to talk. The weather is perfect for this; it's about 65 degrees Fahrenheit and a soft wind blows through the tree branches next to where we are sitting. She asks me how my back and legs are feeling and for the first time in a couple of hours I am reminded of my situation with the sciatica. I shift in my chair and tell her I am feeling fine right at that moment.

I ask her to share her story with me once again. My goal here is to help her reframe what has occurred over the past several years in a way that will serve her for the next decade and beyond. We can all feel like victims at times but it is crucial to move past that as quickly as we possibly can. My sciatica is the perfect example of what I am talking about here. I could allow this setback to define me. Instead I choose to move through it gracefully, knowing that it is only temporary. I also want to learn from this experience to be able to better relate to people with chronic physical and psychological conditions. This will increase my ability to be empathetic and understanding in the future.

She begins to tell her story and I interrupt each time she places blame away from herself and her actions or begins to wallow in what happened to her as the victim in the story. An hour and a half later she tells her story in a very different way and in a tone of gratitude for her experiences, including an almost two year relationship with a narcissistic man who left her feeling empty and alone and short ten thousand dollars in her bank account. She has forgiven him, and herself and chooses to remember the few times they had open and honest communication during their time together. It is so wonderful to be able to help someone move from feeling like the world is out to get them, to the point where they are thankful for what occurred.

I had to do this for myself after I left my teaching job and came online in 2006. For two decades or even longer I had thought of myself as a victim of my circumstances instead of as an active participant in my life situation.

In the spring of 2005 I made the conscious decision to change my life completely. This was exhilarating as well as terrifying and within a year I had learned how and why to take full responsibility for everything that occurred in my life, including the things I could not have possibility caused, such as being diagnosed with cancer, riding out Hurricane Andrew, and being shaken to my core by the Northridge earthquake. If these things were attracted into my life experience then I had to assume the responsibility of at least having some part in bringing that about.

As my new life unfolded I took even more pride in the fact that I was an active leader in what I would experience each day and taking responsibility in this way made me stronger and happier.

In terms of positioning my client as an expert and authority in her new business of working for herself as a virtual assistant, we will use her experiences at her jobs where she worked in customer service and in home health care. Her true gifts are in being able to say just the right thing to people who are confused, upset, and angry and turning that around into helping them to feel cared for and cared about, understood for what they once did not know anything about, and respected for their opinions and beliefs.

It is most interesting to me that all of us want and need these same things from our life experience each day, yet we sometimes allow one unhappy experience ruin our day. For example, you may get up one morning and have breakfast with your family, help get children to school and a spouse to their job, go to work, stop by the shopping mall or grocery store after work, and drive home to meet your family for dinner and time together during the evening. Even if ninety-nine percent of your day went very well, one person saying something rude or unkind can be what you focus on for the next day or two. Wouldn't it be better and far more joyous to focus on the one or two positive things someone said or did that made you smile and to feel good about yourself instead?

Getting back to my client, my goal is to empower her to understand and fully believe that what she is able to do for others is life changing for them as well as for her. A huge part of this is confidence.

When I left my job as a classroom teacher and started my online business my confidence and self-esteem was at an all time low. I was engaging in negative self-talk on a daily basis and finally had to make a conscious effort to turn that around.

Now I exude confidence and work diligently to boost up the people around me to increase their level of confidence.

It's interesting to me that it can take years of positive actions to build confidence, yet one or two people can make negative comments and people will lose their confidence quickly. We must be strong and believe in ourselves enough so that no one and no situation can make us lose this important part of who we are.

I have my client make a list of the accomplishments she has been responsible for achieving in her life, as well as those others helped her to achieve. We dig deep, going back to her years in elementary school when she won the third grade spelling bee. I have her visualize that day, what she was wearing, what someone said, what it looked like in the school auditorium, how it felt when she spelled the first word correctly and how it felt to spell her winning word - voyage. I ask her to do it out loud as she did on that day. She stands up, eyes closed, remembering how it felt on that day more than three decades ago.

"Voyage. V-O-Y-A-G-E. Voyage."

Her eyes fly open and she exclaims,

"My grandmother was there in the audience! It was a surprise and I saw her when I spelled the last word and looked directly out at the audience for the first time that day."

She sits down and we continue. It turns out she has accomplished so much already in her lifetime, both on her own and with the help of others. She laughs and says she focuses much more on the events and situations in her life that did not go as planned than the ones that did, and even exceeded her expectations. I tell her that is common and that we must remind ourselves on an ongoing basis of how powerful and capable we are.

She breathes a long sigh of relief, signaling me to move on to the work she wants to complete by the end of the summer. We dig in and make lists, write down goals, and compile resources and the names of people who will help her with all of this.

All of us meet in the dining room to regroup and make small talk before retiring for the evening. My work is done here, at least for now.

# Section Six - Homeward Bound

*Home where my thought's escaping*
*Home where my music's playing*
*Home where my love lies waiting*
*Silently for me*
~ Paul Simon - "Homeward Bound"

All good things must come to an end and this road trip is no different. It's June twenty-eighth and I have now been on the road for two weeks and a day. Taking into consideration everything I've been through in terms of my injury and all that I've seen and done when it comes to connecting with people, I declare my trip to be a success so far.

I still have three clients to see in Texas, as well as someone I have never met in person but know through an online forum I have been a part of for several years. This will be joyous and an excellent way to experience even more of what life has to offer on my way back home to California.

Today my thoughts are around the idea of being willing to go the distance and make better decisions in your life and business. Speed is not the goal, nor is perfection. I prefer to seek excellence in my life and business and to be just one percent more excellent each day.

I learned this concept of improving one percent each day from thought leader and motivational speaker Brian Tracy. During my first year of self-discovery when I was in transition from working as a classroom teacher and in real estate to leaving that life behind in favor of online entrepreneurship I had the privilege of spending three days with Brian as a part of one of the groups I had joined during the summer of 2005.

He was patient and kind and made everything into a lesson of one type or another. I can remember the exact moment I decided to emulate that teaching style and incorporate it into my own business as it unfolded. We were in a conference room in a resort hotel in Irvine, California and he stepped away from our group of about twenty-five people and on to the platform where he had his laptop set up. He turned on the projector and all bodies shifted and eyes turned towards the screen in unison.

He had been speaking with someone from our group about the power of maintaining a good memory and he jumped at the opportunity for a teaching moment with all of us. He taught us a simple but powerful process for remembering a series of unrelated words by telling a story that connected them. Within ten minutes we had learned the skill of teaching, and selling, by using stories that your student or prospect will connect with by assigning their own meaning to your words.

On that day I vowed to become a lifelong learner with the goal of improving at least one percent each day, and have continued this practice for well over a decade as of this writing. Those one percents add up quickly and this is an excellent strategy to add to your entrepreneurial toolbox.

A thought works its way into my mind as I continue along the highway and it is one around the topic of judgment. Over my lifetime I have considered myself to be a person whose judgment has not always been on track when it comes to interpersonal relationships or business decisions. It has always been so difficult for me to admit these shortcomings, even to myself. Perhaps in thinking this about myself I am simply exacerbating the situation as I further propagate this theory in my subconscious, based on what I have shared around thoughts, feelings, beliefs, actions, and results.

I consider reframing this so that I can improve one percent a day in this area. I review the facts, at least those I consider to be real. When it comes to meeting new people I believe I am not always a good judge of character. Many times a person I would think of as being honest and forthcoming later proves to be someone with too many character flaws to list. Why wasn't I able to see this sooner? Did I assign traits to this person in order to prove to myself they were worthy of my friendship and trust?

When it comes to business, I believe I am not able to see beyond the initial facts presented and that later on I could realize I have made a poor judgment call that will cost me dearly in time and money. What did I miss in the beginning? How can I improve in this area in the future?

With relationships, I honestly believe that ongoing practice and experience with other humans is the best way for me to improve my skills. As an only child and an introvert I missed out on opportunities for "sandbox play" that is crucial to a very young child's development. And my mother suffered from germophobia, rendering the regular act of sandbox play an impossibility.

My friends growing up tended to be two or three years older or younger than myself and thus I successfully avoided some of the competition and tension that is normal with friends of the same age. As an adult there is no age distinction between friends, save for peers and colleagues at work or in groups where this struggle still exists.

My goal as an author and entrepreneur is to put myself in position to interact with others every day so that I have a chance to practice and improve both my social and business skills and to make them more appropriate for the situation. I feel I'm making progress with this on most days.

I consider myself to be more a student of economics than of psychology and must make adjustments in my thinking in order to turn my situation with business judgment around in a positive way. What resources do I have access to that can educate me in an ongoing way?

The answer to this is the Mastermind group I have successfully nurtured for a decade now. These are mostly men and a few women who have an uncanny sense of what is going on with a variety of business scenarios.

When I first started my physical products business on Amazon I went to them to share what I was doing and to ask them some general questions. To my surprise they went specific right away and began asking me questions about the various aspects and moving parts of this type of business. When I inquired as to how they would understand these details and be so insightful when they weren't involved in this type of business they answered that "business is business" and the same or similar strategies can be applied to any situation.

I highly recommend you surround yourself with people who are smarter and more experienced than you are and to create a bond between you so that you may meet with them on a regular basis. They will enjoy doing so, and will also claim to be learning as much from you as you are from them.

# Duck Dynasties and Bumper Cars

*To awaken quite alone in a strange town is one of the pleasantest sensations in the world.*
~ Freya Stark

The next two days go by quickly as I make my way down Interstate 85 into Georgia and the rush hour traffic in Atlanta where it is pouring rain. Then I'm on Interstate 20, headed west for the first time on this road trip and traveling through Alabama, where I stop to spend the night in Birmingham. My intention was to have dinner with business associates who live in Cullman but they are in Birmingham today to see the Broadway musical "Wicked" at the Birmingham-Jefferson Convention Complex. I beg off as the soft motel bed envelops me and I drift off to sleep.

Early in the morning I shower in my handicap access bathroom, dress and get back on I-20 west towards Mississippi and Louisiana. These states are smaller than the ones I drove through earlier in my trip and faster to drive through from end to end. It's still raining hard and I exit in Monroe, Louisiana to take refuge at the Pecanland Mall.

The mall appears to be the center of activity for this city f fifty thousand inhabitants, known for its rich history that began during the Civil War when this area was home to two Confederate training camps. Coca-Cola also traces its history back to when the first bottler of the beverage, Joseph Augustus Biedenharn relocated here from Mississippi in 1913. Biedenharn and his son also founded Delta Airlines later on.

It doesn't take me long to realize I'm in the heart of "Duck Dynasty" country. This was an extremely popular television reality show at the time that has since been discontinued, based on the story of the Robertson family who are engaged in a business which specializes in fabricating duck calls and decoys out of salvaged swamp wood. The company, Duck Commanders has grown from a mom-and-pop operation to a multimillion dollar sporting empire, established in 1973 by family patriarch Phil Robertson (aka the Duck Commander) who invented his famous duck call. It is now run by his business-savvy son, Willie.

People of all ages drift around the mall, pausing here and there before heading towards another store, kiosk, or food counter. Some are wearing their "Duck Dynasty" hats and shirts and in an instant I am transported back to 1978 as I was driving from California to New York to begin my first year in law school.

I'd had a tire blow out not far from Oklahoma City on that road trip and my husband had decided we should have it replaced at the Sears store in the mall. As we waited for the work to be completed we spent some time walking past the stores, window shopping and people watching.

There was a bumper car attraction and even some live country musicians entertaining the shoppers. But what stood out most to me were the people wearing t-shirts with Willie Nelson's name and image on them. In the summer of '78 Willie Nelson was not a household name and we had no idea who he was or what he did. It wasn't until that fall in New York I discovered his music and shared the story with my fellow law students of how I had first heard of him.

I'm eighteen hundred miles from my home in California and galaxies away in terms of my life experience. I am fascinated by the people here and want to know more.

I can hear the rain and thunder pounding and see lightning striking on the skylight in the middle of the food court, and decide to get a bite to eat and see what's showing at the Cinemark Cinema 10 theaters. I settle on "Alice Through the Looking Glass" and think about how wonderful and strange life can be all at the same time as I sink into my seat and the opening credits roll.

# The Creative Process

*Creativity is intelligence having fun.*
~ Albert Einstein

It's only on a carefully planned road trip that we know exactly where we are at the beginning and where we intend to arrive at the end, geographically speaking. Those finite beginning and end points allow us to encapsulate the journey in our mind and have at least some control over our results. These defined points in time, space, and reality can be further manipulated both in the moment and in retrospect.

Entrepreneurship is not like that. It more resembles life, and that is the rub. No matter how detailed or specific or disciplined your daily thoughts and actions are, life still happens. There is no such thing as perfection and striving for excellence must become the goal.

While I was working as a classroom teacher in the inner city of Los Angeles over a twenty year period, I absolutely detested the fact that I was forced to adhere to a strict schedule throughout every single day. The administration made it such that every moment of our time from the second we drove into the school's parking lot in the morning until we backed out and on to the street in the afternoon was carefully accounted for, controlled, and scrutinized. There was no room for creativity or mistakes or life lessons to unfold. Certainly no fun was to be had on purpose. And God help you if the teachers or students did not complete the assigned tasks in the time allotted, and with above average results, at the least.

When I resigned at the end of June in 2006 I was thrilled at the prospect of doing exactly as I pleased now that I would be working for myself as an online entrepreneur. Yet this euphoria would not last as the harsh realities set in.

At first I slept each morning until I awoke on my own, did as I pleased for most of the day, went to bed whenever I was too tired or had run out of activities to keep me interested, and did what I considered to be real work for some period of time in between.

I soon found out his type of relaxed schedule and mindset does not make you very much, if any money. The business only grows and flourishes if you are present, mentally and physically to make it happen. I longed for the structure of a loosely prescribed routine.

By creating a strict yet flexible schedule for myself I was able that summer to lay the foundation for what would become a very lucrative and enjoyable business.

The model I chose to emulate? The one I had learned and become accustomed to as a school teacher for the previous two decades.

That's correct. I set a time to get up each morning, already had a "to-do" list of what I wished to accomplish laid out for the day, and went to bed even earlier than I had on school nights in the past. Sure, there were days here and there when I got off schedule for what I considered to be a good reason. But for most of that summer I was bound by the schedule I had created for myself out of a necessity to succeed.

My road trip was similar in that I had made the decision to follow a twenty-one day schedule and move forward in a way that would serve me, my goals for the trip, and the people I had arranged to spend time with along the way.

Then. Life. Happened.

Having the back pain that intensified over two days and ended up manifesting as sciatica and rendering me helpless was a shock to my system, but even more psychologically than physically. This occurrence brought me back to that summer of 2006 I just mentioned, when I was sure that having a set schedule that was seldom deviated from was the answer to all of my dreams and plans as a new entrepreneur. It sounded wonderful until it abruptly stopped working in my favor. I was forced to step back, regroup, and come to some new precepts around the topic of entrepreneurship and how I would reinvent myself to create the life I so wanted and deserved.

It is said that "the best laid plans of mice and men often go askew." This excerpt below is from a poem entitled "To A Mouse" that was penned by Robert Burns in 1785. The original stanza in Modern English goes like this:

*But Mouse, you are not alone,*
*In proving foresight may be vain:*
*The best laid schemes of mice and men*
*Go often askew,*
*And leave us nothing but grief and pain,*
*For promised joy!*

Later on author John Steinbeck took the title to his 1937 novel "Of Mice and Men" from that same line. And in Douglas Adams's *Hitchhikers Guide to the Galaxy* series, mice are the physical protrusions into our dimension of a race of hyper intelligent and pan-dimensional beings who commissioned construction of the Earth to find the Question to the Ultimate Answer of Life, the Universe, and Everything. When their plans go wrong they lament that "the best laid plans of mice" don't always work out.

So I am in good company here when I reminisce about that time when I had to let go of what had worked so well, even though I despised it from the core of my being, and embraced the concept of "disciplined creativity" that allowed me to change myself and my life from the inside out as I grew my business. We'll return to this thread of thought in another chapter.

Was I more creative than usual during this road trip? Yes, most definitely.

# Lost and Then Found

*Not until we are lost do we begin*
*to understand ourselves.*
~ Henry David Thoreau

I make my way west on Interstate 10 through Lake Charles, Louisiana and on into Texas. Years ago my first husband and I used to remark that a third of our trip from Los Angeles to Miami and back home again as well entailed driving through the state of Texas. Back then the interstate did not go all the way through the state and it took much longer back then than it will for me today. But I also know I'll miss the deer and other wildlife along the sides of the road, and the many small towns along the way where the motel rooms were always an interesting experience and the food could stay with you for days after you consumed it.

Crossing the state line I realize that I'm not sure where to exit. I have planned to meet a lady I met a year earlier in an online forum and am looking forward to it immensely. Pulling over to the side of the road I'm immediately aware of the eighteen wheelers blowing past me. It's making my car shake like it would in an earthquake back in California.

I've gone too far west and have to drive another five miles to exit and turn back east to Lake Charles. The sun is in my eyes as I retrace my steps and I think of that as the punishment for not knowing where I was going when I started out this morning. I make a mental note to be more organized, and another to not be so hard on myself.

When I reach Lake Charles I take exit 33 to highway 171 north to Longville, then highway 190 west to Jasper. It looks like Texas to me, meaning that the brush along the way is what I think of when I picture the Texas countryside. A rabbit dashes across the highway and narrowly misses my front left tire. Thank you, God for sparing this innocent creature on this beautiful day.

In Jasper I veer off the main highway to make a hard right turn to the north to connect with Interstate 20. Then I drive west for another twenty miles or so to exit in Longview. My online friend from the forum, Michelle lives an hour north of Longview and we have agreed to meet at the Cracker Barrel for a late lunch and a long visit.

When I searched for the address using my maps app on my iPhone earlier it came up with this description: "Homey chain restaurant serving American comfort food, with an on-site general store." Yes, that is accurate. I now will have eaten at this chain more than a dozen times during my road trip and I am comforted by the food, the familiarity, and the look and feel of each place.

I park as close to the front door as I can, as my pain has increased today and I'm ready to sit down anywhere in the air conditioning and think about something else for awhile.

Michelle, or Chelle as she prefers to be called arrives soon after I get inside and we exchange a long hug, the kind you give someone when you just know they will become a cherished friend. It's almost two o'clock so we have our choice of tables and choose one facing the parking lot. My whole world is in my vehicle right now and I couldn't bear to lose even one small piece of my now more than ever before treasured belongings.

We make small talk at first. I tell her about the sciatica and why this was the reason I was unable to meet with another lady from our online forum while I was in St. Louis two weeks ago. Two weeks on the road feels like six months and I tell Chelle I'm sure I have aged ten years during this road trip. She laughs politely and does not comment, as she has only seen photos of me online as a reference.

She tells me about her family, a husband who works construction in Louisiana currently, but still comes back home almost every night unless he has to work late. There are two teenage sons from a previous marriage and they are her pride and joy. She was going to bring them but wasn't sure it would be alright with me. I tell her I wish she had brought them along so I could have met them.

Each of her sons is a part of her online business and each boy has a specialty area. She is homeschooling them and we talk about my twenty years in the classroom and why my family chose to home school my grandkids when they saw what the public school experience was like. They even tried a private school for Kindergarten with the eldest but did not care for that either.

The eldest granddaughter is the girl we lost at age twelve and her story is one I am still not able to share. By talking about her in this setting my emotions boil up, but it eases the pain that stays with you for a lifetime.

We are two strangers with much in common, brought together on this humid afternoon at the end of June in a sparsely populated section of east Texas. I am reminded how grateful I am for these experiences that my online marketing business makes possible for me and for entrepreneurs everywhere. If not for that, I would never have the opportunity to cross paths and get to know someone like Chelle. That would be very sad, indeed and quite lonely in the big scheme of things.

She shares her experiences of working from home, connecting with people all over the world, and being a part of a small town where no one seems to understand her. I encourage her to reach out to more people and find the one or two with whom she can experience the friendship she craves. We discuss schedules and plans and products and marketing.

It's the idea of creative discipline that resonates with Chelle on this day and it has been a joy to share these hours with her before getting back in my car and settling in for my drive to the next leg of my adventure.

# Creative Discipline

*A culture of discipline is not a principle of business,*
*it is a principle of greatness.*
~ Jim Collins

By setting a rigid schedule for my new business I was simply going through the paces each day. By this I mean that I was not allowing my creative juices to flow, even a little bit. Too much discipline kept me penned in with what I was striving to achieve. It became a Catch-22 for me in that if I honestly did not believe I was a creative person, why in the world would I develop a schedule that would have flexibility in it for the creative process to emerge?

Successful companies have used this strategy of implementing a "culture of discipline" in order to unleash a plethora of creativity. Our success as entrepreneurs is launched by our imaginations, visions, willingness to take massive risks, leaps of faith, and creative thoughts that are eventually harnessed into tangible assets.

This manner of thinking, believing, and manifesting can get out of hand, and soon the "suits" come in to tame the wild horses. If you work for yourself it's your alter ego that cracks the whip and your creative side jumps to attention.

You focus on turning off your right-brained ideas and bury your head in more sane and logical processes such as checklists, outlines, blueprints, and those dreaded rules. This might work to create order out of the chaos, but in so doing we have also killed the entrepreneurial spirit and what we now think of as the KonMari Method.

This is based on author and organizing expert Marie Kondo's strategies of decluttering the physical and mental with a goal of tossing out the clutter and keeping only what sparks joy in our life. Her first book, *The Life-Changing Magic of Tidying Up* was published in 2014 and gifted to me soon after by a close friend in Santa Barbara who is always a few steps ahead of the trends. Marie and her philosophies are now known the world over. We must find and maintain our individual, unique balance for logic and creativity if our lives are to be fulfilled, I believe.

I made a rule for myself years ago that states "if it isn't fun, I don't do it" and this is true for many people who describe themselves as creatives. In corporations and with entrepreneurs alike, there must be a fun portion of the process or it just isn't worth being a part of any longer. Now that I think about it, this was the very reason that caused me to lose interest in my teaching career over two decades. But I digress.

As the magic wanes the mediocrity quickly slides in on little cat feet and soon the work is similar to any other that one might choose in order to make a living. It represents the death of a dream and can lead to boredom and incompetence.

So what's the solution to this situation, where creative minds butt heads with linear, logical thinking from across the aisle but basically both are on the same page and with similar goals?

You must blend focus and discipline and work ethic into one ball of energy and implementation where the results are outstanding on any level and everyone involved feels like a valuable part of the process. No one is settling for work that only partially fulfills their innermost need for satisfaction and completion.

Strict rules and discipline combine to bring about creativity and innovation. It is sometimes linear but may also be circular. In a company this manifests as shared responsibility for projects, with an emphasis on outstanding results. For entrepreneurs it looks like massive productivity with the possibility of never before seen results, leading to superior products and systems for creating them.

In the corporate world this is referred to as a "culture of discipline" and in the world of entrepreneurship it is thought of as lifestyle design with success.

Experiment, think outside the box, imagine what could be, and then use a proven blueprint to test everything at least three times to make sure you're on the right track for your goal. It's consistency within restraints and the freedom to make magic. It's safe and fun and effective and makes your life worth living just to know you participated in greatness of its own creation.

Like a finely created main dish, the recipe cannot possibly be written down because it will be interpreted differently by each chef who chooses to undertake it and make it their own.

Stay focused and productive each work day, allow creativity to have free reign within a structured framework, and always take full responsibility for both your results and your outcomes.

# Dallas on My Mind

*Texas is neither southern nor western. Texas is Texas.*
~ Senator William Blakley

Spending more than three hours with Chelle was surreal in many aspects. Two women who had only met on the internet because of a shared interest in entrepreneurship and a desire to connect and build relationships, we made the decision to come together in the middle of nowhere in the second largest state in America to see what could come of it.

Now she was headed north to fix dinner for her sons and to see if her husband would be staying in Lake Charles for the night or coming home to her and the boys later that evening.

I need gas and exit Interstate 20 in Kilgore to go to the Gateway Travel Plaza. I maintain my routine of getting out and stretching my legs for at least five minutes whenever I stop and decide to go into the gift shop to see what they have. After just visiting the Cracker Barrel gift shop and picking up a few select items, this place has nothing that appeals to me.

I pay for the gas, carefully get back into my car, and head northwest to my next destination - Dallas. It's just over a hundred miles away, but my navigation system shows it will take two and a half hours. Traffic. Something I haven't seen much of on this trip, but still a part of my adventure.

The comfort food I had for lunch seems to be keeping my pain at bay, or at least that's what I am imagining. I had the country fried steak, boiled cabbage, green beans, and sweet potatoes, with two squares of corn bread on the side. Half of this feast is securely wedged between a pair of shoes and a small box of books on the floor of the backseat, safe in its styrofoam container. We don't have much styrofoam in California, but it certainly is convenient for traveling with food.

Dallas, I'm on my way!

# The Bucket List

*Life is what happens to you while you're busy making other plans.*
~ John Lennon, in "Beautiful Boy"

The traffic increases in number of cars and trucks sharing the interstate with me, as well as in the intensity of navigating from lane to lane. I drive through miles and miles of smaller cities and suburbs before entering the Dallas city limits. I have been here on numerous occasions over the past decade, each time flying in to either the Dallas/Ft. Worth airport or the regional Love Field. I am now so accustomed to flying I refer to airports by their code. Dallas/Fort Worth International Airport is DFW. Love Field is DAL.

I attempt to recall the last time I drove through this part of the country and have to guesstimate is was around 1979. Was Texas always this spread out? Yes, it was and now there are even more people who have made this state their home. When I am in California I seem to forget there are places even larger. Well, a place anyway. Texas is that place for me, as I have yet to visit Alaska. Long ago it was known for having the biggest steaks and hats and other things but now I don't see them bragging about that on the billboards on the side of the highways. Progress changes our perceptions, even if the reality remains the same.

At this stop along my journey I will be driving to the home of someone I care about very much. Her name is Cynthia and we met while I was speaking for the first time at a marketing event in Atlanta in 2008. She made quite an impression on me and we agreed to keep in touch. A couple of weeks later she mailed a personal note to me and asked to join my mentor program. I already had two other people in the group and Cynthia was a welcome addition.

Now she has invited me to stay at her home for two days. I haven't told her about the sciatica and I keep my fingers crossed the house is one-story and I will be able to get in and out of her shower easily.

When I exit Interstate 635 on Walnut Hill Lane I look for a place to pull over. I'm sore and stiff and need a few minutes to stretch my body from the pretzel I have morphed into before going on to her house. Luckily there is a large community park within sight and I pull in to the parking lot and get out of the car. I look at myself in the vanity mirror and in leaning in to do this bring about great pain to my lower back. I silently ask for a do-over and wonder what I was thinking when attempting this now acrobatic move. I begin massaging my leg just above the knee in a routine I have developed over the past week or so that is helpful and makes me relax. Fifteen minutes later I am feeling much stronger and drive the final few miles to my destination.

When I pull into the driveway of her one-story ranch style home I hear the bark of what sounds to be a very large dog. It turns out he lives next door and is simply announcing my arrival. Just as I press "send" on my text to let Cynthia know I have arrived she comes bounding out the front door.

She comes over to the driver's side door to greet me and immediately sees that I am in pain.

"What have you done, lady?"

We hug and she takes my purse away from me.

"Is this thing filled with rocks?"

Cynthia looks great. She has lost some weight and done something with her hair. I stand up straight to feel less frumpy and the pain shoots down my left leg like I have been struck by lightning.

I am blessed to spend time with the most gracious and loving hostess for the next two days. She has the guest room made up for me and waits on me hand and foot. Somehow I believe she would do this even if I was of sound body at this time. It feels wonderful to be cared for in this way.

We work on one of her projects for an hour before she dismisses me with instructions to get into bed and to let her know if I need anything else before I go to sleep.

The following day another one of my students, Ron, drives up from where he lives about an hour south of Dallas to join us for the day. He has a background in physical therapy and silently watches my every move.

We go out for lunch at a Thai restaurant and Ron has me pause by the side of my car. He politely takes my cane from me and adjusts the height a centimeter or so. I can't believe it makes such a difference and we go inside to eat.

Back to the house and we have a valuable and insightful discussion about what derails entrepreneurs from achieving their goals. Why are some people more successful than others and what can we learn from observing our own and other's behavior?

I decide to keep my thoughts on these topics to myself for the time being and assign them tasks that will move each of them forward from where they are today to closer to where they are headed for the short term. "Big picture" thinking is wonderful, but many times you have to get your daily routine in place before you can daydream about your future.

I honestly believe we are all ordinary people attempting to lead extraordinary lives as entrepreneurs. You make that transition from ordinary to extraordinary by taking the million tiny steps required. The average person will give up much too soon to ever get any real traction; the extraordinary person will course correct as often as possible to make their goals and dreams become their reality.

# New Eyes

*The voyage of discovery is not in seeking new landscapes, but in having new eyes.*
~ Marcel Proust, "The Captive", Remembrance of Things Past

On Friday morning, the first day of July Cynthia carries my bags out to the car so I may resume my travels and head towards home. As we share a final hug she tells me that it was on her bucket list for many years to have me stay at her home. I am touched in a way I thought wasn't possible and I thank her for the invitation and opportunity to have spent this precious time with her.

This was my last scheduled stop, and for the first time since starting this road trip I have no specific plan or schedule for my day. I'm a little less than fifteen hundred miles from home and it is calling to me. But I won't rush it as I believe there is still much for me to learn and experience on my journey of self-discovery.

As I drive past the park where I stopped to rest two days earlier I realize that I will miss the fourth of July festivities I was counting on being a part of when I returned to southern California. The early morning parade, the Rotary pancake breakfast, and the barbeque at the Elk's Lodge later in the afternoon will carry on without me this year and I am okay with that. My only goal now is to find some more answers to my questions in regards to life and relationships and entrepreneurship as I travel west to California.

Interstate 635 south will take me to I-30 west. Eventually, somewhere around Fort Worth that will become the I-20 and finally I-10 will take me into Los Angeles before I connect with the I-210 north to the I-5 north. It sounds complicated but is not. Our system of highways and interstates in the United States is perhaps the most logically laid out plan I have encountered in my world travels, give or take a few quirks here and there, which we many times take for granted.

For now, the wide open spaces serve as fertile ground for my thoughts to expand and congeal as I complete the final segment of my road trip. At this point it's awesome to conceive of the fact that I have accomplished so much under the challenging conditions that unfolded for me. In retrospect I wouldn't have wanted it to be any other way, as we only grow and transform when we are met with opportunities or hardships we had not and could not have anticipated in advance of them occurring.

I get into the rhythm of driving and thinking and land on the topic of bright, shiny objects, called BSOs for short.

Back in late 2005 and into the spring of 2006 I found myself getting caught up in the BSO trap. I had been warned against this "A squirrel!" thinking, but when you are just beginning it is so easy to get caught up with things that seem simultaneously to be so appealing and filled with possibility. For me it was Google AdWords, AdSense, membership sites, niche sites, and ghost writing.

Perry Marshall was the expert on AdWords at the time, so I purchased his book at my local Border's bookstore. This was before Amazon offered books for sale and we actually enjoyed going in to a bookstore and browsing the shelves. I still do, and you may as well but many have closed as our world continues to change. I am fortunate to live in two cities that each has independent bookstores.

Perry's book was almost a thousand pages long and over my head after the first two chapters. He offered an online course along with the book and I signed up almost immediately.

Joel Comm was teaching AdSense strategies and I purchased his book to learn how to set up websites that would sell products based on the advertisements that magically appeared throughout the site.

Membership is still a mystery to the online marketing community and out of reach for most of us due to the cost and technical skills required. It would be two full years before Stu McLaren and Tracy Childers would create Wishlist Member, a membership site plugin available for WordPress sites. I would have the honor of watching this unfold as I was in a Mastermind with them during this time and beyond.

Tiffany Dow, who now goes by Tiffany Lambert, is the authority when it comes to ghost writing in the internet marketing space. She has written content for some of the biggest names in our industry, including John Reese, Ewen Chia, and Rich Schefren, just to name a few.

She has become known for creating niche sites and matching content and is active on a very popular and now defunct site called Squidoo.

I stop for lunch in Abilene, after seeing the sign for a Cracker Barrel right off Interstate 20. There's a gas station almost right next to it where I will fill up my tank on my way back to the highway after I eat. I had hoped to check out the Beehive restaurant further down the road but don't feel strong enough to experiment today.

Chicken fried steak, okra, mashed potatoes, and buttermilk biscuits. Yes, please bring me a box to take some of this with me and bring the check any time. Three minutes of small talk to find out my waiter is named Frank and he isn't sure what he will do after he stops working for Cracker Barrel someday.

I recommend taking a class at one of the many colleges in Abilene. Frank shares that he wanted to go to Texas State Technical College but he doesn't think he is smart enough to make it. I suggest taking one of their online courses and he lights up with his small rendition of joy at this discussion. I tell him I know it can be scary to start college. I understand what it's like to have a dream but not have family support.

They didn't have online classes when I was his age - we both laugh at this revelation - and when you're online no one sees if you're struggling with the course work. I tell him I believe in him based on what a great job he is doing as a waiter. He smiles a little wider than before and promises to look in to it. I leave him with "you'll never know unless you try; it doesn't matter what anyone else thinks; and it's worth the time and financial sacrifice to have a life you want and deserve."

I have memorized this routine and hope that some of the people I speak with are inspired and motivated to make some serious life decisions as a result.

Now I will have something for dinner before I go to sleep tonight in my accessible motel room in Pecos, Texas. One more day in Texas and then I'll feel like I'm making some progress in my westerly direction.

I sit in my car in the parking lot before driving next door to get gas. That's when I see a young woman, not more than twenty-five, I'm sure getting out of her van. I get goose bumps now just thinking about this and how it affected me so deeply.

Every movement is labored and I'm not sure what to label her condition, or even why I feel the need to as this processes through my mind. Humans seem to need labels to identify and remember things, like toddlers and preschoolers do when they are learning about the world around them. I'm at a loss as I grasp for a label here so I abandon the notion.

My hand slowly slides off the door handle and back into my lap as I decide this is not the time to get out of my car. In comparison to the struggle I am observing with this young woman, I feel like a fraud. My situation, as bad as it seems to me right now, is temporary. I know this is not the case for the young woman.

She eases out of the driver's seat and gets her footing before moving slowly and awkwardly two steps back to open the side door panel. Then she pulls out a shiny red walker and grabs hold. Next is her purse, which she places in the small basket at the front of the walker. Once she has everything she needs in just the right place she closes the doors and makes her way up the ramp towards the restaurant. Every step is deliberate and measured. One misstep could have major repercussions.

There, but for the grace of God, go I. In that moment I am having a transformational experience

Tears stream down my face and suddenly I am out of my car and making my way up the ramp. Even at my slow pace I am able to easily get to the front door before she can and I smile at her as she gets closer to me.

I hold open the door to the restaurant and she smiles at me. More like a grin and I see that she is even younger than I thought when I had first spotted her from across the parking lot.

"Thank you kindly, ma'am," she says.

"Of course. What's your name?"

"Emily. My name is Emily."

"I'm Connie. Is there anything else I can do?"

"Tell the Lord I need to move a little faster, Connie."

She is now inside and moving towards the restrooms.

"Have a wonderful day, Emily."

I back out of the restaurant slowly to make sure she is making progress to get to the ladies' room.

Emily. That is the only label I need for this person I have had the pleasure of connecting with.

I make my way back to my car and the pain shoots down my back and into my left leg. I know the pain will be excruciating as I hoist myself into my seat. But something is different now. My world is different now. I am different now.

I get it. I finally get it.

My life is a gift. Every day is a gift. This pain is a gift. I let the tears that have welled up in my eyes flow down my cheeks so I can see well enough to drive over to the gas station just a few hundred feet away. As I pump the gas I feel the life coursing through my veins and know that every moment is a gift and I will make every effort to not waste any of my gift ever again. No more feeling sorry for myself; I'm done with that. This precept will take time to percolate and I look forward to thinking and writing about the thoughts and feelings I am experiencing at this moment.

Back on Interstate 20 now, heading west to Pecos. It's two hundred fifty miles from Abilene and instead of driving sixty miles an hour to get there in four hours I go more slowly to enjoy the drive. I am amazed at how much more I can see and take in when I'm going fifty miles per hour. I wonder what I'm missing that could be seen better if going forty. Those sharing the road with me would not appreciate that and I speed up to fifty again.

My exit is Highway 285 north and I pass Sonic Burger, Kentucky Fried Chicken, and Burger King as I make my way along the desolate highway. Then there's Wal-Mart on the left and my motel, Holiday Inn Express on the right.

The lady at the front desk doesn't make eye contact more than once, carefully checking me in while glancing at my car with California plates. Then she checks my driver's license for a full minute before asking for my registration so she can match it to the plates on my vehicle.

I imagine her wondering why a disabled woman driving all alone this far from home has chosen her motel. If she would have asked I would have told her the story; I prefer something clean and quiet and not right off the interstate. And I'm frugal - no, I'm cheap - and the price of $89 for the night sounds right.

But she doesn't ask and I don't share as she hands me the key card and points to my room, two doors to the right.

I have my purse and cane in one hand and my box of food and a bag of clean clothes in the other. I won't need my laptop and feel confident about leaving it the car overnight. The room is clean and has a shower I can easily get in and out of in the morning. I'm asleep before dark and I dream about the best way to use my gift of life now that I have become so awakened and aware of it in my life. I leave Pecos at dawn on Saturday morning, July the second.

# Thinking of Home

*Twenty years from now you will be more disappointed by the things you didn't do than by the ones you did do.*
~ Mark Twain

Just west of Pecos Interstate 20 merges with Interstate 10 and I head to El Paso for a lunch break and to fill up my gas tank. Again the gas prices are higher than I expected for them to be in Texas, but then my perceptions were not based on any research and therefore not reality.

My memories of El Paso include the time when my mother and I took the train from Los Angeles to Miami when I was eleven years old. I still have the black and white photo she took of me standing next to the train, wearing my Dale Evans cowboy jacket and pink cowboy boots and holding a favorite stuffed animal. The city seems more modern now, but I guess it would after more than forty years.

I'm thinking of home today and feeling both nostalgic and homesick for the first time in three weeks. I long for the comfort of familiar places and faces, as well as my own bed. I miss my animals terribly and wonder if they have given up on me ever returning.

This is the first time I have thought about turning this road trip into a book. But I'm not so sure it would be of interest to anyone who does not know me personally, or is connected with me through my previous books and online business. Perhaps I can share relevant stories for newer entrepreneurs and strategies for first time authors. Obviously, I made the decision to write this book and I sincerely hope you are getting something from it that will affect you in a positive way.

Authorship is a whole new ballgame since self-publishing became open to everyone through Amazon's publishing options. I readily acknowledge I would not be a bestselling author had this visionary company not taken the route they did around 2008 and I am forever grateful. My life and my business shifted on the day I became published.

When I wrote and published my first book, *Huge Profits with a Tiny List: 50 Ways to Use Relationship Marketing to Increase Your Bottom Line* in July of 2010 my world would be forever changed.

Overnight my speaking engagements increased and I was included in a variety of online projects that would have eluded me previously. It was as though I had been invited to a private club where I was the newest member. I became totally immersed in this world and by the end of the summer of 2010 I had already outlined my second and third books I would publish within the next year.

My reference point came from my academic days, where professors lived under the "publish or perish" philosophy. The continued pressure to publish academic work in order to succeed in an academic career is the dark side of higher education, in my opinion.

Ongoing, successful publications bring attention to scholars and their sponsoring institutions, which can help with continued funding, as well as their careers. Scholars who publish infrequently, or who focus on activities that do not result in publications, such as instructing undergraduates, may lose ground in competition for available tenure-track positions.

While the world of entrepreneurship has no such demands, requirements, or even suggestions, I decided to take full advantage of this opportunity to make a name for myself in a different way and to separate from the pack, so to speak.

When John Wiley & Sons publishing house contacted me in 2011 I was flattered they even knew my name. They had just recently opened an office in Dubai and it was a British editor working in that office who first called me. After a few months of conversations, leading to early negotiations I respectfully declined their offer. Going with them would mean giving up the rights to some of my content and my online courses based on my books so it didn't make sense at that point. I then created my own publishing company as Hunter's Moon Publishing and that is how my books continue to be published in both print and digital formats.

Publishing over twenty full length books, so far is an accomplishment I am extremely proud of, and working with new authors to help them achieve their time freedom and financial goals is an important mission for my life's work. My intention is to create an oeuvre as a legacy for those who seek to know more about the topics I have become expert in over the years.

I had planned to make it to Tucson, Arizona for the night but decide to only go another fifty miles to Las Cruces, New Mexico and spend the night there instead. I am so weary and it would be enjoyable to have some time to rest and take things at a slower pace. I'd actually like to see a city I'm in for a change, instead of simply passing through. And then I'd like to go home.

# Las Cruces

*Imagination is more important than knowledge.*
*Knowledge is limited. Imagination encircles the world.*
~ Albert Einstein

It's about five in the afternoon when I enter the city limits of Las Cruces. I haven't called ahead to reserve a room and decide to check out the La Quinta Inn on Avenida de Mesilla. The man at the front desk smiles and introduces himself.

"I'm Floyd and I'm the manager. From the looks of things I will guess you do not want the deluxe King Suite I have on the second floor. Is a smaller room with a double bed two doors down to the left alright with you?"

I can't quite detect his accent but it is a delightful sound. Perhaps upstate New York with a touch of semi-rural South Carolina.

"Yes, I am grateful for your kindness," I hear myself saying. He walks me to the room and tells me I can park in the handicapped space right in front without having a placard for my car.

"I'm kind of in charge of that sort of thing here on the property." He tips his wide brim hat at me and I disappear inside the room.

The truth is that a smaller room is better for me right now. Less distance from the front door to any other area and a feeling of coziness that is comforting. I fall asleep thinking about the warmth of human kindness and how this experience is one I wouldn't have wanted to miss during my lifetime.

I'm up at dawn and type out an email to my community with details of where I am and what I am doing. It includes a free download of one of my books through Amazon's Kindle Select program, offers to two of my courses, and two more for other people's products I am an affiliate for so I will earn a commission on each sale. I'm tempted to share a little about the personal side of this trip, about the sciatica and how it has changed my perspective since leaving southern California almost three weeks ago. But I leave that for another time. Time; something that can be fleeting or drag on forever.

Last night I went online to see what there was to do in Las Cruces today. Horseback riding and the Prehistoric Trackways National Monument are out, as is the Lake Valley Historic Mining Town.

The New Mexico Spaceport Authority sounds enticing, but is perhaps too adventurous for me on this day. I happily settle on the Las Cruces Railroad Museum. It is housed in the Sante Fe Depot, which is listed on the National Register of Historic Buildings.

For several hours I am almost feeling back to normal, back to the person I was before this sciatica invaded my personal space and took over my life. But my attitude and outlook has shifted and now I am grateful simply for being alive.

For the first time since arriving in St. Louis I am anxious to take photos of my surroundings. The train exhibits will make for lasting memories. I sit down periodically, hanging my cane over my arm as I have become accustomed to doing. It's interesting how humans can adapt to almost any situation when the need arises. I guess this is how we have evolved over time and are still on the planet. Our ancestors endured greater hardships than I can imagine, so surely I am up to dealing with my current predicament.

I offer to take photos of couples and families and they excitedly hand me their phones with the camera at the ready. The younger people give me some instructions and I politely listen and nod. Some offer to reciprocate but I decline with a smile.

There is a gift shop that leads into the cafeteria. I am impressed with this marketing that forces visitors to see all of the souvenirs and knickknacks they have for sale before we can get something to eat or drink.

A young man greets me and shows me to a table near the cash register. He offers to come back and take my order so I won't have to go through the line. This is very thoughtful and I thank him profusely. I order a tuna salad sandwich, a side order of fruit salad, and a bottle of unfiltered apple juice. I hand him my credit card and refrain from my tired joke about not going to the shopping mall on his way back.

My next stop will be three hundred miles due west on Interstate 10. This drive will take me through the Gila and Coronado National Forests, as well as through several Indian Reservations as I leave New Mexico and enter Arizona. I have also left the Central time zone and come back into the Pacific time zone for the first time since leaving home three weeks earlier.

A light rainfall turns into blinding wind and rain. I stay in the right lane and keep pace with the other drivers until I see an exit sign. At the end of the ramp I slow down to stop at the traffic light. Right or left, which way should I choose?

# Choices

*It's our choices, Harry, that show what we truly are, far more than our abilities.*
~ J.K. Rowling

Life is all about choices. As a young child those choices are made for us by our parents, older siblings, and other family members.

As we approach school age teachers and other adults come in to the mix. At some point we are given the responsibility of making our own choices, small ones at first and then bigger, more important ones. We practice succeeding and failing with older and more experienced people ready to praise us when our choices lead to positive outcomes and to catch us when we make a decision that isn't in our best interest.

I think back to what I was taught while I was in law school in New York so many years ago. In my classes on torts I learned that according to common law jurisdictions a tort is a civil wrong that causes a claimant to suffer loss or harm, resulting in legal liability for the person who commits the tortious act. This can include the intentional infliction of emotional distress, negligence, financial losses, injuries, invasion of privacy and many other things. The person who commits the tort against another is referred to as the tortfeasor.

In English common law there is applied the law of sevens, which states that a child under the age of seven is not capable of having the capacity to be responsible for their torts, minors aged seven to fourteen are presumed to lack this capacity, and those older than fourteen are held to have the same capacity as adults. There is ongoing debate on this topic and the individual must be taken into consideration, but in a court of law in the United States the precedent has been to stick to this law of sevens across the board.

Why am I bringing this up and how does this relate to entrepreneurship, you may be asking? I'm glad you asked.

As adults we must take full responsibility for the choices we make and the ensuing results. If you are at a job your employer will make many choices for you. When something does not work out the way it was intended it is common practice to blame the employer rather than the employee.

This area was the basis of an ongoing power struggle while I was employed as a classroom teacher with the Los Angeles Unified School District. The focus was on test scores.

When a specific teacher's class did not test at an acceptable level the administration was quick to blame the teacher. Job security was threatened. The teacher's Union would then pass the blame on to the school's principal and other site administrators. There were no winners and ruffled feathers did not settle over time. I had the experience of working at one elementary school for six of my twenty years that was in the bottom five percent in the entire district for standardized test scores for each of those years. Placing blame simply added to the situation and little was done to make changes.

My argument throughout this time was that I would be willing to take full responsibility for my test scores under certain conditions. These would include having at least seventy-five percent of my class be comprised of the same students on the first day of school as on the last.

Also, I wanted some flexibility in how I could teach these students, instead of being forced to teach "by the book" (created by administrators and others who typically had not taught in the classroom for many years) throughout each day. And finally, I wanted to be able to incorporate music, art, and other "soft topics" into my curriculum and to bring back science fairs and to add new technology. Of course, these ideas fell on deaf ears and the madness continued, at least in the inner city of Los Angeles where I was teaching.

As an entrepreneur you are the primary decision maker in everything related to your business. My results are measured in a variety of ways, including the quantifiable ones related to my productivity based on number and amount of sales, prospects joining or leaving my database (list) over a specified time period, and the number of products and courses I create, books I write and publish, and trainings I complete.

Then there are the numbers that cannot be quantified. These would include those related to making choices simply because it *feels* like the right choice at the time. For example, my goal each month is to write and publish new posts to each of my two primary blogs, one at ConnieRagenGreen.com and the other at HugeProfitsTinyList.com. But I do not commit to a specific number of posts. Instead, I wait until I have something to say on a topic within the area of online marketing and mindset and then I begin to write.

Choices can be based on objective or subjective factors and both are equally as important to the final outcome and results you will experience. The crucial point here is to take action by making choices based on what you know right now. Eliminate "analysis paralysis" and keep moving. Realize that by doing nothing you have made a choice. Choosing something moves you closer to success.

Instead of sitting at the traffic light and waiting for it to go from red to green to red again because no one is behind me to force my into making a decision, I choose to turn left and see what this little town of San Simon, Arizona has to offer a weary traveler caught in a heavy rainstorm.

# Mentoring on the Road

*We make a living by what we get,*
*we make a life by what we give.*
~ Sir Winston Churchill

It turns out that San Simon is a census-designated place in Cochise, Arizona, just like Crozet, Virginia was. That was the community I was in just over a week ago with my client and her family. I find this to be an interesting coincidence, considering that I had never heard of census-designated places, or CDPs until making this road trip.

There are only one hundred sixty-five inhabitants in San Simon. There are a few buildings on either side of the street I am driving down, Cochise Avenue. I pass the San Simon Volunteer Fire District and turn left on 6th Street. This is the I-10 Business Loop and now I am heading west once again. When I pass the U-Haul dealer and the Chevron gas station I realize I am at the edge of town and decide to pull into the parking lot on my right to wait out the rainstorm.

I take this time to rearrange my back seat. This is where I have three baskets; one for clean clothes, another for dirty laundry, and the one in the middle for maps and other important notes and papers.

It is then that I realize I have entered Pacific Time and have a call scheduled with Maria, one of the people I mentor. Before leaving California I told them to stay in touch and schedule calls with me while I am driving. I have Bluetooth set up to be hands free and know this will be beneficial for them while also helping me to pass the time. I do some of my best thinking while I am on the open road, I have discovered.

While sitting in my car in the parking lot of the U-Haul dealer, listening to the almost deafening sound of rain slamming against the walls of the pre-engineered steel building I dial Maria's number. I recognize this as being a "Butler Building" from my life decades ago when I was married for the first time and my husband was a general contractor. So many stories come to mind but they are not relevant to this story so I will keep them close for another time.

Maria answers right away. She lives in Orlando, Florida and is anxious to discuss her business with me. Her overall niche is real estate and more specifically, helping retired people invest in single family and multi-unit properties in college towns in the southeastern part of the United States. This would include Florida, Georgia, Tennessee, Alabama, Mississippi, the Carolinas, Louisiana, and parts of Texas.

This positions her as an expert in an area where there is high demand for people who are known, liked, and trusted to share their knowledge and expertise in the form of information products and online courses.

### Information As a Product

The fastest and easiest foray into the world of online entrepreneurship is through the selling of information. Yes, it is readily available to anyone with an internet connection and a computer or smart phone, but sifting through the plethora of information and honing it down to the specific details you are searching for can be a daunting and time consuming task.

Enter the online entrepreneur, ready to do the work of researching, curating, and packaging the information into a consumable format and you have a viable business model.

At some point in during the first half of the twentieth century we entered an era that would be referred to as the "Information Age" and our lives would never again be the same.

Now we are in what is referred to as the "Knowledge Age" and all of us are a part of the knowledge economy. This is the use of knowledge to create goods and services. For example, I use my knowledge to create the products, courses, and programs I sell in my business.

A key concept of the knowledge economy is that knowledge and education can be treated as either of these:

A business product, as educational and innovative intellectual products and services can be exported for a high value return or;

A productive asset.

I consider all of my products, courses, and programs to be valuable assets, in that I am able to sell them 24/7/365 in digital format and earn income immediately over the internet.

The term *knowledge economy* was made famous by visionary business consultant Peter Drucker in his 1969 book *The Age of Discontinuity: Guidelines to Our Changing Society*.

For companies, whether online or brick and mortar, intellectual property such as trade secrets, copyrighted material, and patented processes become more valuable in a knowledge economy than at any time earlier in our modern world.

My client, Maria is using this concept of the knowledge economy to earn an excellent living in real estate without having to buy, sell, or develop real estate of her own. Her knowledge is what her clients are investing in. Anyone can position themselves as an expert in their niche market or field and build a similar business.

Mentoring people who are dedicated and focus is what I live for in my business. It was Oprah who said "A mentor is someone who allows you to see the hope inside yourself." My goal with each client is to help them see the hope they possess inside their heart and mind, as well as the genius, innovator, and visionary they are destined to become.

I enter the freeway once again and drive west, south-west another hundred and twenty miles into Tucson.

# The Small Differences

*The moments we have with friends and family, the chances we have to make even a small difference, all those wonderful chances life gives us, life also takes away. It can happen a lot sooner than you think.*

~ Larry Page

This part of the southwest all looks the same to my untrained and unfamiliar eyes. It's Saturday, the second of July and I have another hundred miles to go to get to Phoenix. I will spend the night there and then drive another hundred fifty miles to Blythe, California where I will have lunch with longtime friends I have known since we were all in college together at UCLA so very long ago.

Randy and Jen hit is off right away when they first met during our first quarter together in the fall of 1974. We had an economics class together every morning, as well as a study hall two afternoons each week. When you spend that much time with people during an experience like attending UCLA as an undergraduate you get to know each other pretty well.

He made it clear from the very beginning he would be returning to Blythe to take over the family farm once he graduated. Randy was the youngest of three brothers and the only one who had dreamed of following in his father's footsteps since he was a small boy.

Every day when we had lunch at one of the campus eateries he would regale us with stories from his childhood on the farm. Some of them made Jen and I long for the farm life, while others left us wondering what Randy saw in it that made him so adamant about giving his life to this world. It was one that could be quite lucrative, but also lonely and very cruel at times.

At Thanksgiving Jen joined Randy at the farm for the long weekend. When I had asked her privately what her family thought about her not spending that time with them, she shared that her family consisted of an alcoholic father and an angry older brother. Her mother had abandoned the family years earlier and she had counted the days until she could move away. A high school counselor took an interest in her and helped her apply to and be accepted at half a dozen universities in California. She had chosen UCLA because Los Angeles was the one furthest away from where she had grown up. That was Sacramento, a city in northern California about four hundred miles away.

Upon our return to classes the Monday morning after Thanksgiving she and Randy announced their engagement. His family had fallen in love with her as he had and they decided to commit to each other and to the farm for eternity.

Even though I had married at a young age I knew that my relationship would never be as strong as theirs already was. It was quite a beautiful thing to observe from my perspective. They seemed to complement each other in every way and enjoyed each other's company. We remained the best of friends through graduation and that summer of 1977 I was part of their wedding and celebration.

After a good night's sleep at a Hampton Inn in Phoenix I am on my way down Interstate 10 to meet up with my friends. It's been almost ten years since I have seen them, and that was only briefly when we met for dinner in Los Angeles before they set sail for a cruise to Hawaii.

When I exit the freeway I note the long dusty roads on either side of me. I could not imagine myself ever living near here, with nothing to do or see and the terrain not changing. It's so different than my world in Santa Clarita and Santa Barbara.

Blythe is an agricultural community of just over twenty thousand residents. The climate is typical of the California desert, with extremely hot summers and mild winters.

They greet me on their tractor at the end of the long driveway. Looking like they just walked off the set of "Hee Haw," a popular variety show than ran in syndication during our years together at UCLA, they are wearing matching coveralls and straw hats. Randy is taller than I remember and Jen is thin with muscular arms.

Has it really been thirty-nine years since we graduated and they got married? For a moment I lament my circumstances; me on my own and them closer than ever. Any sadness I am feeling is quickly washed away as we have a group hug before I get back in my car and follow them back to the house.

By the next morning we have all committed to not going more than two years without seeing each other in person ever again. I love how they still include me in their lives after all these years. During the past twenty-four hours I have seen all four of their grown children and bounced the two youngest grandchildren on my knees.

The rocking chair is particularly comfortable and my pain is minimal. I almost don't want to get up, but the road is calling and I am ready to head home. But Jen pulls me up out of the chair and tells me she and Randy want to show me something before I go. Earlier I had overheard their eldest son saying that one of the cows was sick and the vet had been called, but I didn't think that was what they wanted me to see.

We climb aboard the bed of a full size pickup truck, driven by one of their ranch hands. As we pass acres of cotton and melons and their seventy head of cattle Randy points out various things to me.

"I know it probably all looks the same to you, Connie, but when you make this your life you are able to see the small differences in everything."

He waves his arms high and low, and from front to back to give his words a more dramatic effect. Jen is smiling and nodding in agreement.

They both go on to tell me how they can tell when a crop is ready to be harvested simply by smelling the air. They can tell each cow apart because no two look the same. And they know what day it is, or at least which week without having to look at a calendar because of the small differences they have internalized over the years.

Jen takes my hand in hers and we smile lovingly at one another before she speaks. I think back to those first days when we had met at UCLA. Randy and Jen had spotted the small differences each of them had and turned them into a life together.

"It's the small differences that make this life so special, don't you agree?"

I nod in agreement with her, looking up at Randy and shading my eyes from the bright sunlight so I can make out his features. I know that I will spend much time rolling these words over and over in the recesses of my mind, sifting through the grains of wisdom and finally understanding a little more of this concept in the coming days. Jen's voice has a mellifluous tone I could listen to forever. Again, just when I think I have a firm grip on life, someone appears to remind me I still have much to learn.

As I drive away from the Palo Verde Valley along Interstate 10 (this highway is officially the Christopher Columbus Transcontinental Highway) I decide to enjoy my last two hundred fifty miles by taking my time to get home. I'm an hour into my drive before I realize it's the fourth of July. When I exit to get a snack and some gasoline I see banners announcing the local events for the holiday.

When I get back in the car I think about how this tank of gas will carry me through to my home in Santa Clarita. I've kept track of every detail of this trip in the little notebook I keep in the car. I'm pretty sure this is my twenty-third tank of gas, but I don't take out the notebook to check for sure. There will be plenty of time to do that once I am back at home.

# No More Cheap Gas

*My past is in the rear view mirror;*
*my future is right in front of me.*
~ Connie Ragen Green

The next several hours are surreal in that some of them fly by at warp speed while others are in slow motion and in another dimension. I can't feel my legs but somehow I am driving.

I miss an exit with a gas station on either side of the interstate and decide to just keep driving until another one appears. There it is, but the prices are posted and I get sticker shock when I see how much it is. I'm driving through Desert Center, California and decide to go a little further to find some lower prices. They're sure to be up ahead.

Another hour and the gas is even more expensive. I laugh out loud, thinking about the reputation I have for being frugal with myself and generous with others. There will be no more cheap gas during this trip and I don't have enough in the tank to make it all the way home.

At some point my mind begins to wander and I am reliving these past three weeks. I am not the same person who headed east; my transformation began mentally before I was stricken physically. So many lessons for me to internalize. So much to think about and understand. Every day brought more joy and more challenges.

What if I just kept driving, past Santa Clarita and the home I have called home since 2006, and then past Santa Barbara, the other city I have called home since 2012. I could go north along the coast on turn inward to Interstate 5 to reach central, and then northern California. More people to meet and situations to encounter.

I glance into the rear view mirror and realize that what I see represents my past. Then I stare out the front windshield and welcome my future.

# That's My Exit

*My fuel tank is below empty, but on this day*
*my heart is filled to the brim.*
~ Connie Ragen Green

As I exit the Antelope Valley freeway at Sand Canyon Road I slowly exhale. I'm less than twenty minutes from home and feeling a joy that I will attempt to explain. The gently curving road allows the landscape to reveal itself in its own time, one section at a time. A short stretch of sycamores summon me in their direction; a group of older homes sit closely together, as though forming their own village; a neatly trimmed hedge lines the side of the road, sheltering the avocado trees from the dust and exhaust fumes.

I turn off the main road and in to my neighborhood, driving well below the speed limit to enjoy these last few minutes of my road trip. It's July 4th and everything is eerily still on the streets leading up to mine. Coming almost to a stop I pull in front of a house about five down from mine and park so I can think and set my intention for the next segment of this day, where I will walk through my front door and hug my family members.

As I sit there I glance into my rearview mirror and once again see my past behind me. All of the miles on all of these days; the many people and experiences; the totality of my thoughts and the revelations that unfolded are all a part of my DNA now. Nothing could ever be the same again. I am filled with love and joy for nature and all mankind.

The engine started once again, I put the car into gear and inch forward. I'm almost out of gas it seems. How did that happen? Now I can't remember this last day on the road. My tunnel vision and blinders got me home, so I am thankful and not so hard on myself for the last hundred or more forgotten miles. Yes, I had lunch at a fast food place several hours ago but I'm not sure where or about any of the details. I give myself permission to just "be" for today.

As I limp past the houses and turn into my driveway a feeling of extreme peace washes over me.

Has it only been twenty-two days since I backed out of this driveway to embark on this adventure? It feels more like a hundred and twenty-two to me. I'm now a different person in many ways, and the same ol' me in others. In my fragile state I'm not sure what was real and what was imagined while I was on the road.

Swiftly I am transported over to the day I arrived in St. Louis and looked up at the two story brick building Hans was calling home. At that moment I was so very proud of his accomplishments and sad that I could not enjoy those days with him more fully. But it was in full gratitude that I allowed him to serve me by carrying my bags up the stairs and down again, preparing the delicious food from his home country of China, and drawing the bath that I would not be able to lift my leg high enough to step into.

Now I am in Virginia, deep within the forested outskirts of Shenandoah National Park at the home of my client and her family. I can hear the birds singing and the unrecognizable sounds of creatures deeper in the woods. The sounds, colors, and smells were otherworldly to me and I feel some tears sliding down my cheeks. The innate senses can be powerful madeleines, bringing up strong, voluntary memories from times past, though these are inevitably partial.

I sit in the driveway with my eyes closed for another few moments, tipping my head back and sinking deep into the seat. I'm still on my road trip until I open the car door. Now I am being whisked away to Texas, a big state filled with people who have big ideas and even bigger dreams. My clients there showed me enormous love as they catered to my needs and accepted my help with their businesses.

I open my eyes and all is familiar to me again. My house on my street is beckoning to me and I know there are people inside who are anxious to see me again and hear all about my adventure. They didn't know about the sciatica or the hardship I endured as a result, as I didn't want them to worry needlessly. Soon I will tell them everything, but today is not the day. I am too weary to share anything right now.

With extra care I open the car door to exit my vehicle, dragging my purse over my right arm with my cane attached to my left arm. Even though it's only about four meters to the front door each step is more laborious than the one before. The key is in the lock and before I turn it to the right to unlock the door I hear my dogs barking. What a joyful sound! Then I'm inside and greeted by two family members.

"What have you done?" one says.

Without a word I limp into the guest bedroom a few feet past the front door and carefully lie down on the bed. Someone removes my shoes and takes my purse and another helps me to slide beneath the covers. The lights are switched off and the door is gently closed behind them. The sounds of my little dogs barking their greeting to me fade off into the distance. I will dream of my road trip and feel grateful to have had this experience. It is my hope that I will never forget a moment of what occurred during my journey.

# Epilogue

*We may look the same on the outside, but once we have expanded our minds we are never the same.*
~ Connie Ragen Green

While I was on my cross country road trip I never dreamed I'd be writing a book about it later on. But writing about my life's experiences is who I am, so this book was destined to be written.

The trip changed me in many ways. It had been a journey of self-discovery, for sure and this wouldn't end when I arrived back home. What do I mean by this?

A "journey of self-discovery" refers to a travel, pilgrimage, or series of events whereby a person attempts to determine how they feel about themselves and their priorities and of becoming aware of one's true potential, character, and motives. For me this meant thinking more about the big picture of my life and business instead of being caught up in the details. It included a renewed commitment to excellence and to being tolerant of the people and situations that I found frustrating in the past.

Time passed. My sciatica pain diminished, but not right away. It would be four months of physical therapy and a walking regime I created to help me heal without drugs or surgery. Small things I had taken for granted, like going back upstairs when I had forgotten something would never be viewed in the same way. Some people in my day to day life in both Santa Clarita and Santa Barbara didn't even know I had been gone for three weeks. Others knew and asked me how it went.

I would mention the trip in passing but the details became less vivid over time. A blog post gave the overall story but not in an emotionally powered way.

Two weeks after my return I was on my way to Europe for my month long visit I take each year to spend time with extended family members in Finland. Physically this trip is a difficult one for me, but I insisted on my family doing everything they had planned. I'm more than happy to sit on a bench and wait for them if I am unable to take another step at any point in time. I stopped in London to speak at a writer's conference and remember the kindness of strangers as I boarded the flight to Los Angeles from the tarmac. People did everything but carry me up the stairs so I could keep moving.

When I returned from Europe I again revisited my trip and attempted to make sense of the feelings I was experiencing. I found myself humming one song over and over again as summer turned into fall. It's called "It Goes Like It Goes" and was written by David Shire (music) and Norman Gimbel (lyrics) as the score for the 1979 film "Norma Rae." This was the verse in my head:

*So it goes like it goes like the river flows*
*And time it rolls right on.*
*And maybe what's good gets a little bit better*
*And maybe what's bad gets gone.*

I do not know why this song became so meaningful to me. I thought back to the year 1978 when I was working at a bank in Sherman Oaks, in a section of Los Angeles known as the San Fernando Valley. David Shire was an almost daily customer and he and I developed a friendship. He would always arrive around noon and one day we had lunch at Solley's delicatessen next door. It was fun and it became a regular thing for us to meet.

It was during one of these friendly lunch dates that he shared some details about the divorce he was going through with a well known actress. I listened and interjected my thoughts when he went silent. He trusted me and I never betrayed that trust. A month later I left the bank to return to college and we never said goodbye.

Time grows more precious as we clock more hours on our life journey. And it is this time that allows us to grow and shift and change our thoughts, feelings, and beliefs to obtain the results we desire. I think about the wasted time I have spent over my lifetime and decide to reframe that as time used as a tool to teach me what I needed to learn.

And I am here reminded of a quote from Marcel Proust I used earlier in this book:

*"The voyage of discovery is not in seeking new landscapes, but in having new eyes."*

Time is more about learning to see things differently than to simply continue to see new things. Seldom during our lifetimes do we give ourselves the gift of time. Time alone, to ponder and dream; time within a group, where we can learn and grow; or time within our mind to expand and stretch and break through the walls we build in our imagination.

My road trip allowed for all of these and I came home a different person than the one who left. Yes, I had seen many new things, but I had also begun my internal process of seeing things in new and creative new ways. The two simple acts of backing out of my driveway on the first morning and pulling into that same driveway three weeks later serve as bookends to my journey of self-discovery.

# About the Author

Connie Ragen Green is a bestselling author, international speaker, and online marketing strategist who is dedicating her life to serving others as they build and grow successful and lucrative online businesses. Her background includes working as a classroom teacher in the inner city of Los Angeles for twenty years, while simultaneously working in real estate as a broker and residential appraiser. In 2006 she left it all behind to come online, and the rest is history.

She makes her home in two cities in southern California; Santa Clarita in the desert and Santa Barbara at the beach. Connie also spends time in Finland with extended family members and has adopted this country as her second home.

In addition to her writing and work online, Connie consults and strategizes with several major corporations and some non-profits, as well as volunteering with groups such as the international service organization Rotary, the Boys & Girls Clubs, the Benevolent Protective Order of Elks, the women's business organization Zonta, SEE International, and several other charitable groups.

As the recent recipient of the Merrill Hoffman Award, presented to Connie by the Santa Barbara Rotary Club, being honored with this award has strengthened her resolve to serve others around the world in any way she is able to by using her gifts, talents, and experiences in a positive and sincere manner.

Take a look at all of her titles since 2010 at http://ConnieRagenGreenBooks.com and visit her main site at https://ConnieRagenGreen.com.

Made in the USA
Coppell, TX
24 January 2020

14938151R00089